THE HENLEAZE LAKE STORY
An Account and the History of
Henleaze Swimming Club

Compiled from the club's archives
With help from erstwhile members, the authors' albums,
personal experiences, and an ear to the ground

Derek F. Klemperer and Joyce F. Klemperer

Photoprocessing Mark J. Thompson

First published in 2007

ISBN 978-0-9555531-0-3

British Library Cataloguing-in-Publication Data
A catalogue record for this book is available from the British Library.

Published by Redcliffe Press Ltd, Bristol
Typeset by Harper Phototypesetters Ltd, Northampton
Cover design by Mark Cavanagh
Printed and bound by HSW Print, Tonypandy, Rhondda

Copies of this book may be purchased from the superintendents at Henleaze Lake or from the authors at 25 Rockside Drive, Bristol, BS9 4NU. Tel: 0117 962 3748, email: derek.klemperer@virgin.net

CONTENTS

Fig. P.1 An aircraft's view of Henleaze Lake around 1930. Henleaze Swimming Club is well ensconced with its changing rooms, polo nets and diving tower but the surroundings are still rural. However, the Lake Road houses have been built up to number 69 and suburbia is coming. Compare the 1996 aerial view shown in Colour Fig. P.1.

PREFACE

Henleaze Lake, the property of Henleaze Swimming Club, is situated three miles north of the centre of Bristol at Grid Reference ST 580774. It is a narrow, steep-sided quarry approximately 450 metres long that is full of water fed by small springs in the side and floor of the quarry. When full, the lake holds about 50,000 cubic metres (11 million gallons) of water. The average width of around 30 metres gives a total water area of 1.35 hectares (3.3 acres). The northern end is two to three metres deep, shelving gradually down to the southern end where the depth is five to six metres.

The deep end is surrounded by lawns and willow trees and it is used by members and their guests for swimming, diving, and sunbathing during the summer. Fishing takes place the year round, there being access to the waters edge right up to the northern end. The total area of the property is some 3.6 hectares (9 acres), the land area being much larger than the area of water.

When limestone quarrying ceased in 1912 the quarry was allowed to fill with water and it became known as Southmead Lake. Only later did it acquire the name Henleaze Lake. After some years of public use swimming in the lake was placed on a proper footing by the formation of Henleaze Swimming Club in 1919. The club adhered strictly to the rules of the Amateur Swimming Association. It first leased the lake property and then, in 1933 the club was able to buy the entire property.

This is an account of Henleaze Lake and Henleaze Swimming Club from the earliest quarrying days through to the beginning of the twenty-first century. We shall tell the true story of a magic place, warts and all, and include the immediate surroundings of the lake property where this is relevant. Fig. P.1 and Colour Fig. P.1 show aerial views of Henleaze Lake and its surroundings, the photographs taken some 65 years apart.

CHAPTER 1
THE PRE-WAR YEARS

The things we did last summer, I'll remember, I'll remember all winter long
Popular song, 1949

Southmead Quarries

There were many limestone quarries in the north of Bristol during the seventeenth, eighteenth and nineteenth centuries. The A to Z street directory with its Quarry Roads, Lanes, Ways and Steps bears testimony to this quarrying past and in many places one can still see limestone cliff faces that have been left by the quarry workers. The quarrymen were accommodated in cottages and terraces, some of which have survived; their appearance is a give-away. Limestone quarrying was the only major industrial activity in Westbury-on-Trym. Early in the nineteenth century the Southmead Quarries were split into two when Eastfield Road was built to increase access to the workings and to the lime kilns. In 1860 Eastfield Terrace was built to house the quarrymen and five lime kilns are marked on the 1903 Ordnance Survey map (Fig. 1.1).

Two of these lime kilns still exist in a state of disrepair at the corner of Eastfield Road and Henleaze Road (colloquially known as 'Clark's Corner') and the most northerly one of the five survived until 1938 when it was demolished by Henleaze Swimming Club. The quarry south of Eastfield Road became known as Eastfield Quarry and most of this area is now Old Quarry Park. The quarry immediately to the north of Eastfield Road was filled in and partly built upon in the 1930s. Tennis courts stood here for many years to be replaced more recently by Merlin Court. The part of Southmead Quarries further north is now Henleaze Lake; it became the property of Henleaze Swimming Club in 1933.

Eastfield Quarry

For over 300 years the area which is now Old Quarry Park was an active limestone quarry. Fig. 1.2 left shows local historian Ray Pepworth MBE at the entrance to one of the old kilns. In these kilns layers of quarried limestone were alternated with layers of wood and, when full, the kiln was fired to produce calcium oxide. The oxide was 'slaked' with water to produce the lime which was and still is used extensively for builders' mortar. Records show that the wills of three local lime-burners who died in the seventeenth and eighteenth century left estates worth 12 shillings, £15 and £20. The old quarry office still exists at Clark's Corner with a porch over the door marked Business Office (Fig. 1.2 right). Other quarry buildings and the flooded quarry in 1936 are shown in Fig. 1.3. Chock Lane in

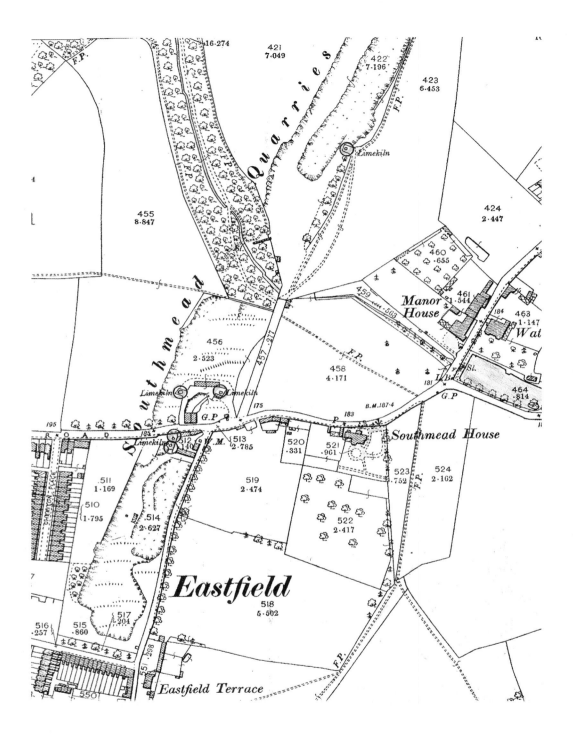

Fig. 1.1 The 1903 Ordnance Survey Map of the Southmead Quarries area. The quarrying of limestone was a major industry. Most of the limestone was burnt to produce builders' mortar. The five lime kilns in the area are ringed. (reproduced from the O.S. map, Bristol Record Office)

Westbury-on-Trym, then Chalk Lane, was forever white from carts carrying loads from the lime kilns.

In 1916 coal used for machinery to crush the limestone and for pumping out the spring water became so expensive that the pumps were stopped and the springs took over, eventually giving a maximum depth of water of 30 metres. The Clark family moved to Clark's Corner in 1927 when John Clark was 11 years old and the flooded quarry level was 10 metres below the wall on Henleaze Road. It was then a

Fig. 1.2 *Left:* Ray Pepworth, local historian, in the entrance of one of the two old lime kilns at Clark's Corner, the corner of Eastfield Road and Henleaze Road photographed in 1999. Limestone was quarried here during the 17th, 18th and 19th centuries. *Right:* The door to the business office of the former Eastfield Quarry at the corner of Eastfield Road and Henleaze Road photographed in 1999. The corner site is now a yard for A.P. Clark & Son, Paving and Surfacing Contractors since 1890. (photos Derek Klemperer)

Fig. 1.3 The flooded Eastfield Quarry and quarry buildings in 1936. (photo John and Dorothy Clark)

Fig. 1.4 John Clark and friend rafting on the flooded Eastfield Quarry c. 1930. The quarry was filled in with refuse and Bristol blitz rubble during the 1940s and the site is now Old Quarry Park. (photo John and Dorothy Clark)

wonderfully peaceful and picturesque lake with calm spring water and surrounded by trees. Fig. 1.4 shows the young John Clark rafting with a friend and a dog on the lake where he spent many hours swimming and fishing. When the water was low – as in 1934 – it is said that the iron gates at the entrance to a former lead mine could be located. The tunnel went under what is now the yard and curved round to the East under Eastfield Road.

Another place where it was possible to swim *al fresco* at about this time existed in the garden of The Manor House on the west side of Southmead Road. It is marked as a swimming bath on the plan that was prepared for the 1926 auction, in three bits, of over 9 acres of The Manor House estate. In 1926 a boating pond also existed on the opposite east side of Southmead Road where Waterdale Close now stands.

In 1930 Bristol Council purchased Eastfield Quarry for tipping and started filling it in from the southern end but swimming and boating continued throughout the 1930s. In those days one thought nothing of swimming in open water that contained refuse! The 1936 Ordnance Survey map (Fig. 1.5) shows the partially-filled Eastfield Quarry and the tennis courts north of Eastfield Road. Eventually the lake was completely filled in with refuse and rubble from the Bristol blitz during World War Two. One older resident in Henleaze Terrace still recalls the 1930s style refuse lorries backing up to the former quarry and discharging their loads.

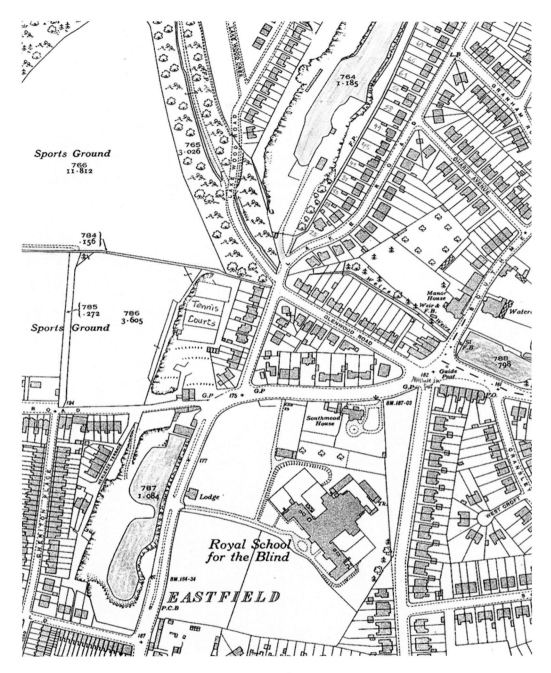

Fig. 1.5 The 1936 Ordnance Survey Map of the Eastfield Quarries area. The flooded Eastfield Quarry south of Eastfield Road has been partially filled in. Houses and tennis courts have been built on the site of the former quarry just north of Eastfield Road. (reproduced from the O.S. map, Bristol Record Office)

The Blind School

The Royal School of Industry for the Blind in Henleaze (Fig. 1.6) was built on the opposite side of Henleaze Road from Eastfield Quarry and opened in January 1911. The school had spacious grounds and a chapel at which local residents were welcome. After World War Two Henleaze Swimming Club held its committee meetings and AGMs at the school and visiting teams of competitors were accommodated there during gala occasions. The dwindling number of pupils (a reflection on medical advances at that time) meant that facilities could be extended to the nearby swimming club and a close association arose. When the school launched an appeal to fund the construction of a swimming pool in its own grounds, both the Western Counties Amateur Swimming Association and Henleaze Swimming Club in its own right made generous contributions.

An attractive open air pool was duly built and opened in 1950. Local children were invited to use the pool with the Blind School pupils during the summer months. Many children, including the authors' children, had their first swimming lessons in this pool. In 1969 the Blind School site was sold and the school building was demolished to make way for housing; the pool was filled in. Today one can still trace its outline on one of the open green spaces. This is one of the open-air swimming pools that Bristol has been steadily losing over the years; others are the

Fig. 1.6 The Royal School for the Blind in Henleaze was situated on Henleaze Road opposite Old Quarry Park. Visiting teams for galas at Henleaze Lake were accommodated in the building. The school opened in Henleaze in 1911 and was sold to make way for housing in 1969 after pupil numbers had fallen dramatically from a peak of 110; it was finally demolished with explosives in 1971. (M.J. Tozer collection)

Bristol Lido in Fishponds which was filled in in 1974 and the Victoria Open Air Pool in Clifton which closed in 1990. It is good to note, however, that there is nationally an awakening of interest in saving the UK's ageing lidos. Bristol has also been losing indoor pools – Speedwell pool and Filwood pool closed in 2005, but Community Leisure Centres are beginning to replace them.

Swimming in Bristol has been given a boost by the government's national sports initiative aimed at helping more school children learn to swim and by the opening of private health and fitness centres. The Next Generation Club with both indoor and outdoor swimming pools opened close to Henleaze Lake in 2002. A 1981 pool at Filton Leisure Centre was rebuilt and opened in 2002 as a modern indoor swimming pool. The new indoor swimming facility at Horfield Sports Centre which opened in 2005 replaced the antiquated Bristol North Baths which had closed earlier in the same year. Bristol Henleaze Swimming Club, sister club to Henleaze Swimming Club, had trained for many years at Bristol North Baths; training sessions were then perforce moved to the Horfield Pool and to Clifton High School Pool.

Henleaze Lake

The disused kiln at Henleaze Lake can be seen in two photographs taken after quarrying ceased in 1912 (Fig. 1.7) and in about 1931 (Fig. 1.8). This kiln was later dismantled and the material was used to build up the sides of the lake and to construct the polo referee's walkway which is shown in Fig. 1.9. The remains of this

Fig. 1.7 An early photo of Southmead Bathing Pool taken after quarrying ceased in 1912 and the quarry was allowed to flood. The lime kiln on the right of the photograph was used to convert quarried limestone into builders' mortar. The stone dam in the foreground with a track over the top probably served to keep flood water out of the workings while the main part was being pumped out continuously. (M.J. Tozer collection)

Fig. 1.8 A raft race at Henleaze Lake c. 1931. Note the old lime kiln behind the spectators. The lime kiln survived until 1938 when it was demolished by Henleaze Swimming Club and the stone was used to build up the lake banks. (photo unknown)

Fig. 1.9 This photograph, taken during a polo match at Henleaze Lake in about 1949, shows the referee watching play from a special rock walkway that was constructed. Parts of this walkway still exist. (photo Fred Allard)

Fig. 1.10 Water polo was a regular feature at the lake in pre-war years. This old photograph shows the Henleaze Water Polo Team that won the Amateur Swimming Association's Western Counties Junior Water Polo Championships in 1924. Judging by the medals on display the team members enjoyed many other successes. The captain, Cecil Clark sits at the front in the centre. He went on to become President of the ASA 36 years later cp Fig. 1.12. (photo Peter and Hilda Leishman)

rock walkway can still be seen opposite the referee's leaning rail on the other side of the lake when the water level is low.

Water polo was a strong feature in the club's activities in the pre-war years. The 1923 polo team photograph (Fig. 1.10) shows how seriously the players took their sport.

The entrance into the quarry during its working years was via a tunnel situated behind the present pump house. The archway over the exit from this tunnel can still be seen (Fig. 1.11 left). The early maps show this tunnel which is now used to pipe both sewage and water pumped out of the lake into the main sewer on the far side of Lakewood Road. The remains of the quarry men's shot holes can be seen on the rock face at the lake where explosive charges blasted away the limestone (Fig. 1.11 right). Some of the oldest houses in Henleaze were built with stone from this quarry as well as innumerable walls in the area, although all the best limestone went into builders' mortar. Quarrying at Henleaze Lake ceased around 1912 when the quarry filled with water from the underlying springs. Apocryphal contemporary accounts

Fig. 1.11 *Left:* The arch over the entrance tunnel used by the quarry men in former times. It is situated behind the club's pump house at Henleaze Lake. The Lake Road entrance to the site was opened later. (photo Derek Klemperer) *Right:* One of the numerous shot holes left in the former quarry walls at Henleaze Lake. After the hole had been drilled an explosive charge would be set off in the bottom of the hole to blast the hard rock apart. (photo Mark Thompson)

state the men just had time to cut the horses free and run. The flooded quarry became known as Southmead Lake and it was, at that time, surrounded on three sides by fields.

Sir Stanley Hugh Badock (1867–1945)

Stanley Badock (Colour Fig. 1.1) was a prominent businessman in Bristol with a special interest in social work. His mother Miriam Badock was a schoolmistress who founded Badminton School for Girls at Westbury-on-Trym. His father William Badock bought The Manor House on Southmead Road in 1877 and lived there until his death in 1892 when The Manor House was sold. William Badock and his wife Miriam are buried in the same grave in the churchyard of Westbury-on-Trym Parish Church. The Manor House is close to Henleaze Lake (an area that was included in The Manor House estate) and the young Stanley Badock must have known the quarry well. During his father's 15-year residency in The Manor House Stanley Badock grew from 10 to 25 years of age. He married Edna Pethick two years later. The marriage produced three daughters.

In 1905 at the age of 38 Stanley Badock bought Holmwood house and its estate. Holmwood was built in 1803 and the estate adjoined The Manor House estate. He rebuilt a part of the house and linked the gardens with those of The Manor House. Stanley Badock died in 1945 and Holmwood was sold to National Children's Homes. It is now Holmwood House Nursing Home at the top of Channels Hill in Westbury-on-Trym. The Manor House has become The Manor House Nursery at

145 Southmead Road. The stone gate posts still bear the engraving THE MANOR HOUSE.

During World War One Stanley Badock commanded the 6th Gloucester (Volunteer) Battalion, retiring in 1918 with the rank of major. He joined the University of Bristol Council at its foundation in 1918 and became its treasurer and subsequently its chairman. In 1922 he became Pro Chancellor of the University and in 1927 he was awarded the University's degree of Ll.D. honoris causa. Professor A.M. Tyndall wrote that he 'was unquestionably the most active of all the lay members of the Council during the first fifty years of the life of the University'. During his lifetime Stanley Badock was also devoted, with his wife Edna, to congregational church and social welfare work and he was prominent in commercial and civic affairs. He was knighted in 1943. After his death in 1945 his body was cremated. The whereabouts of his ashes are not known. His name is perpetuated in the University's Badock Hall of Residence, the University-endowed Sir Stanley Hugh Badock Chair of Music, and in Badock Woods which abut the west side of the Henleaze Lake property. The woods were originally a part of the Holmwood estate.

Fig. 1.12 The 1924 Executive Committee of Henleaze Swimming Club with some of the early club trophies. These people are all club pioneers *par excellence*. From left to right, back row: Col. H Curley, W.M. Good, W.H. Parr, A.G. Hasler, G. Edwards, T.G. Smith, A.G. Carter, C.D. Milsom, and Frederick W.A. Clark. Front row: Miss Blanche 'Bunny' Clark, Cecil F. Clark, A.P. Furze, W. Scantlebury, R.D. Kidd, G.H. Chivers, and Mrs W.H. Parr. (photo Peter and Hilda Leishman)

The Beginning of Henleaze Swimming Club

After quarrying had finished at Henleaze Lake, Major Badock, the then lessee, stocked the lake with trout (and possibly some crucian carp too) so that he and his friends could enjoy boating and fishing on the lake during his life time. Part of the lake was leased to Mr Curtis who opened it for bathing but when a youth was drowned Major Badock stopped the lease and the lake was closed for swimming.

Albert Wain (Fig. 1.13), who by this time had enjoyed a few years swimming at the lake, had the idea of forming a swimming club with strict A.S.A. rules and regulations. Together with other keen swimmers informal meetings were held and public appeal was ascertained; a large number of swimmers expressed enthusiasm. Major Badock was sympathetic to the idea and was willing to place the lake at the disposal of any responsible club. He was, however, emphatic that certain rules should be adhered to.

Fig. 1.13 Albert Wain, a founder and first honorary secretary of Henleaze Swimming Club. He was elected as the first honorary life member of the club in 1923 and died in 1957. (photo Albert Wain)

He insisted on a full-time caretaker being employed, particularly on Saturdays and Sundays when, Major Badock stated, 'there will be many unauthorised persons coming to bathe and it is also a time when the ill disposed portion of the population inflict much wilful damage on private property'. He also insisted on safety appliances being installed and, thirdly, was most adamant that only good swimmers should be admitted stating: 'It is no place for non-swimmers or beginners and I wish this to be strictly enforced'. This insistence has been perpetuated in the club's first Rule which states: 'The club shall be for swimmers only and shall be known as The Henleaze Swimming Club'. This was again confirmed as recently as the Opening Letter for the 82nd season, dated February 2000, which states that non-swimming children and babies are not permitted to enter the lake grounds and that no non-swimming guests will be admitted. In a letter dated 22 May 1919 Major Badock also states that Sunday bathing should cease at 10.30 a.m. as 'I do not want church-going people to feel we are offering attractions during service hours'. This instruction reflects how seriously Stanley Badock and his wife Edna took their membership of Highbury Congregational Chapel (now St Mary's, Cotham) where Stanley was a deacon. Indeed, after Lady Edna Badock died in 1961 a tablet was placed on the west wall of the chapel recording that they 'worshipped here for sixty years'.

A well-attended preliminary meeting was held in April 1919 and a committee was formed to make arrangements for calling a General Meeting of prospective members of the new club. This meeting was held on 5 May 1919 at St Michael and All Angels' Parish Hall, Gloucester Road. Membership 'took off' and so, from the enthusiasm and inspiration of a few people, Henleaze Swimming Club was born.

The rent was £10 per season and Major Badock states in a letter dated 18 February 1920 'if the sunken boats could be raised you could have them cheap'. He also advises the committee to carry on with the canvas changing screens or tents which were not always waterproof, adding that any wooden structure put up in the future would have to be protected from destruction during the winter; judging from his experience it would be wholly removed for fuel before the spring! Major Badock had obviously witnessed much vandalism.

The first membership card (Fig. 1.14) was issued in 1919 with Colonel George A. Gibbs, MP as President and Major Stanley H. Badock as one of the Vice-Presidents. Mr Albert G. Wain was the first Honorary Secretary. The hours of opening were 6 a.m. to 5 p.m. Monday, Wednesday and Fridays, 6 a.m. to sunset Tuesdays and Thursdays, Saturday 6 a.m. to 9 a.m. and 2 p.m. to sunset and Sundays 6 a.m. to noon. There was one caretaker/superintendent.

In 1920, a year after the club was founded, it was affiliated to the Western Counties Amateur Swimming Association, the Gloucester County Amateur Swimming Association, the Royal Life Saving Society and the Amateur Diving Association. It has remained affiliated to the first three of these bodies to the present day. The Amateur Diving Association became a part of the Western Counties ASA in 1937. The club's Regie Macfarlane, a First World War infantry veteran, was much involved with the ASA at this time. Known to his contemporaries as Mr Diver, he was elected President of Henleaze Swimming Club after World War Two. All the presidents of Henleaze Swimming Club are listed in Appendix 1.

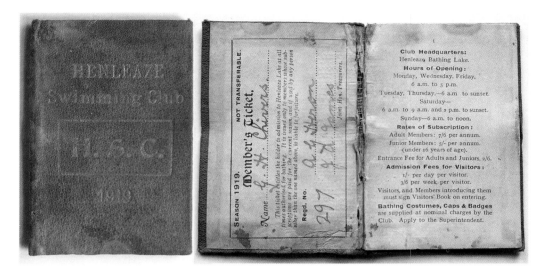

Fig. 1.14 The first membership card for Henleaze Swimming Club, founded 1919. The practice of putting the names of all the club officers onto the membership card persists to this day but the inclusion of holders of club championships and the club rules was dropped after 1969.

The swimming club progressed with much zeal (Fig. 1.12) until May 1924 when information was received that the lake and adjacent properties would be put up for sale by public auction. Anxious committee meetings were held and whilst the club had insufficient funds available it was nevertheless decided to try to secure the land. This attempt, however, was not successful. Assuring news soon came that Major Badock was the purchaser from whom the club then obtained a five-year lease. At the end of this period he kindly granted a further five-year lease.

On 12 May 1933 the lake and surrounding land could finally be purchased from Stanley Hugh Badock (Doctor of Law, Justice of the Peace) by Arthur Furze (bank manager), William Scantlebury (merchant), John Dobson (Professor of Greek), and George Chivers (accountant) acting for Henleaze Swimming Club for the sum of £480.00 to be held by them upon trust. Dr Badock did, however, continue to keep part of the lake (now the fishing area) for the exclusive use of himself and his friends for boating and fishing during his lifetime and he continued to insist on the first rule of the club given above. In the 15th Annual Report of 1933 the Chairman placed on record the committee's thanks to those members who so willingly responded to the appeal for subscriptions to the Purchase Fund.

Two further small pieces of land were purchased by the club in 1935 and 1941 respectively. This land lies on either side of the sloping entrance drive. The purchases enabled the club to move its entrance gate up to Lake Road, cp Fig 4.7 in Chapter 4.

Fig. 1.15 Skating was a popular feature during pre-war winters when sustained hard frost was much more common. These were occasions for the sport and conviviality of summer months to be continued. (photo Ruth Moreton)

The Early Years to the Outbreak of World War Two

During these years the swimming club continued its activities with great enthusiasm. The cash statement for 1929 shows a skating receipt of £35. Skating in the winter (Fig. 1.15) was a regular feature, about 9 inches (22½cm) thickness of ice being required for safety. According to *The Daily Telegraph* in December 1938, skating regulations were governed by a sliding scale, the safe thickness of ice varying with the depth of the water. Where the water was less than four feet deep, as in London's Regent Park Pond, the ice only had to be three inches thick. Clearly the deep water at Henleaze Lake was an important feature in determining when one could skate. Nevertheless ice hockey, as Fred Allard recalled, was played many times in those pre-war years.

During the summer months many open water championship swimming and diving events were held. The lake galas included local, county and international championship events. Fig. 1.16 is an interesting photograph taken during a gala at the lake in the 1920s. It shows the original wooden tower with diving stages at various heights. It is sad to note that nowadays such a venture would never get past the drawing board. The original diving tower was still in use on 3 April 1922, the day the lake opened for the 1922 season. On this occasion a diver was photographed by the press performing from the top stage under harsh weather conditions (Fig. 1.17).

Fig. 1.16 A Gala at Henleaze Lake in the 1920s. The diving tower is the first at Henleaze Lake and it has been replaced twice. Note the ladies' changing marquee and the spectators' cover for viewing the polo matches. This photograph was placed on endurance certificates issued to junior club members. Hats appear to be *de rigeur*. (photo Fred Allard)

The press caption states there was not a large attendance although there was at least one hardy member who braved the snow and sleet! The diving tower was replaced later in the 1920s by a more substantial wooden tower with diving platforms at the correct heights for competition diving.

At about this time the ladies' changing marquee was also replaced with a surplus World War One hut that has been variously described as having been a first aid post or a troop billet (Fig. 1.18). When a party of junior schoolchildren was being shown round the lake in 2005, one of the boys asked if there were still any rifles inside! Although this hut has been refurbished a number of times its appearance is unchanged and it continues to serve as the ladies' changing rooms to this day.

Concern for safety and encouragement of life saving skills is reflected in Major Stanley Badock's early steerage of the swimming club. In 1922 he gave the club a cup that was thereafter awarded annually to the winner of a life saving contest. Many club members gained Royal Life Saving Society awards including Fred Allard (Fig. 1.19) who remained a pillar of the club until his death in 1999 at the age of 97. In 1930 the club won the Society's National Men's Club Challenge Shield. In 1928 a daring rescue at Henleaze Lake by William Harley was brought to Major Badock's attention. The account of this rescue (Fig. 1.20) states that he gave work to William Harley who was unemployed, which may not seem to be important in these days of social security but in 1928 it could well have been a lifeline.

In these pre-World War Two years there were polo matches, swimming, diving and club championships, a learners' section at Bristol North Baths, galas, medals, cups, life saving awards and dances. There was even a club magazine called *The Tough Nut*. In 1932 (the first year for which we have an Annual Report) 35 polo matches were played, the highlight being a match against Cambridge University. Club flannel dances were introduced and proved to be very popular occasions at

A PLUCKY BATHER.

The popular lake of the Henleaze Swimming Club was opened yesterday. Although there was not a large attendance, there was at least one hardy member who braved the snow and sleet. This is not, however, the first time members have dived off the stage this year, for some have attended before the opening day—evidently to practice for the competition for the Times and Mirror Diving Cup.

Fig. 1.17 An unknown diver performs from the top stage of the original wooden diving tower on 3 April 1922, the day the lake opened for the 1922 season. He must have been a hardy individual to brave the snow and sleet. Evidently dogs were not excluded in those days. At the time, this photograph was published in the *Bristol Times and Mirror* and in *The Clifton Chronicle*. After a lacuna of many decades, both these local newspapers have reappeared although *The Clifton Chronicle*'s reappearance in 2006 was brief.

Fig. 1.18 The ladies' changing rooms in 1997. This is a surplus military building that was purchased by the club after World War One and has served the ladies continuously since then, surviving unscathed except for a hole that was burnt through the floor by vandals who lit a fire inside in January 1989. The shutters and the notices are concessions to modern times. Pictured is Grahame Moss, who banks 3000 cheques a season and handles the superintendents' PAYE, sitting as usual in the sun. He often hides behind a newspaper which, if you look closely, may well be upside down. (photo Colin Hannan)

which the girls could get to know the boys. The dances were held in the pavilion at the zoological gardens – until high spirited revellers let the monkeys out one night. St Peters church hall became a convenient venue later on. The club tie and the blazer shown in Colour Fig. 1.3 would be in evidence at these functions, as they also were on gala days at the lake both before and after the war (cp Fig. 2.14 in Chapter 2).

In 1932 the club started awarding annual scholarships, tenable for two years, to six boys and six girls under the age of 15. The boys and girls were selected by a swimming competition but social class was preserved by limiting the entrants to scholars from a number of named Bristol schools and 'clergy daughters'. The scholarships, which carried club membership and free tuition, were awarded annually up to the outbreak of the war.

Fig. 1.21 is a view up the lake in the early 1930s. The water level is high and it must have been a big shock when in 1934, a year after purchasing the lake, the lake water had largely disappeared by August during an exceptional summer drought (Fig. 1.22). This drought, which followed two dry winters, left hundreds of fish

Fig. 1.19 Fred Allard 1902–99, a pillar of Henleaze Swimming Club for 68 years. He held many positions as a club officer and trustee over several decades and possessed a deep knowledge of club information and anecdotes. In 1985 Fred moved into a top floor flat at Willowbank sheltered housing overlooking the lake and produced several watercolours of the lake whilst living there. His ashes lie buried at Henleaze Lake and his is one of four memorial benches that commemorate club worthies. This photograph was taken on Fred's 90th birthday. (photo Peter Allard)

struggling for existence in a few muddy pools. They were taken out and released into the River Avon. Undeterred, however, the Executive Committee took full advantage of the opportunity of the low state of the water to undertake the huge task of cleaning the bottom of the lake and removing some of the rock obstructions.

A low wall was built across the width of the lake at the swimming limit to prevent mud flowing into the pit below the diving tower (Colour Fig. 1.2). The south end of the lake which narrowed and extended for some distance towards the entrance gate was walled off and then filled in to create a car park and a sun bathing lawn. The line of white painted stones which now divides the car park from the lawn is actually the top of a buried wall that once formed one side of a wide stone dam shown in old photographs of the quarry (cp Fig. 1.7). The top of the buried wall forming the other side of the dam can still be observed running parallel to the white stones a couple of metres into the car parking area.

In spite of the drought, competitions continued unabated in 1934 with 49 polo matches being played at the lake, at Bristol North Baths, and at away venues. The men's swimming team proved themselves to be the fastest in Bristol for the eighth year running. Flannel dances were held on the eve of the Annual Gala to entertain

19

RESCUE BY MR. WILLIAM HARLEY — HENLEAZE LAKE 1st MAY 1928.

William Harley, who was walking along the top of the cliffs of Henleaze Lake, heard screams of distress, and running a considerable distance he saw a lady in the water in difficulties. He merely cast off his shoes and without hesitation plunged from the cliff, a height of approximately 30ft. and rescued the lady by carrying her some 40 — 50 yds, where he was able to cling to a ledge of rock until help arrived.

Harley ran a considerable risk from the danger of submerged rock when plunging, and also that there was very little chance of effecting a landing.

At the time, Wm. Harley was an unemployed Labourer with a Wife and five children, and Major Stanley H. Badock, LL.D. J.P., very kindly gave work to him (believed to be only temporary).

Mr. George Edwards, President & Hon. Treasurer, of the Henleaze Club, opened a subscription list and has been instrumental in collecting approximately £16.10.0. for Harley's benefit.

Fig. 1.20 This account of a daring rescue at the lake in 1928 was kindly given by Jean Harley, the rescuer's daughter. The rescue would certainly have attracted the award of a Royal Humane Society medal these days.

the Cambridge team and a second dance took place at the end of the season. Extra galas were held when county and Bristol championships were fought over and the whole ethos of the swimming club during the 1930s was geared into all the various swimming championships. Water polo too was always a strong feature during these years. First class teams such as Cheltenham, Weston-super-Mare and Cambridge University were frequent visitors and one could always rely on seeing one or more polo matches on Saturday afternoons and on mid-week evenings.

Fig. 1.21 View up Henleaze Lake in the early 1930s. The wooden diving tower was replaced in 1950 but the men's changing facility is still exactly the same today. There was no shortage of water in the lake when this photograph was taken cp Fig 1.22. (Doug Satherley collection)

Fig. 1.22 The water in Henleaze Lake largely disappeared during the summer of 1934. A photograph of the empty lake used to hang in the Eastfield Inn on Henleaze Road where committee meetings were once held. The opportunity was taken to clear rubbish from the bottom and, amongst other artefacts, a number of false teeth were found. (photo Fred Allard)

Fig. 1.23 'Pete' Desjardins, the world champion diver, gave demonstrations at Henleaze Lake in 1935 and 1936. These demonstrations attracted huge crowds of paying spectators. Several of the photographs of 'Pete' Desjardins diving were produced as postcards by the club. No one seems to have worried too much about third party liability risks. (photo Fred Allard)

The galas in the 1935 season proved to be exceptionally successful. A highlight was the visit of 'Pete' Desjardins, the Olympic diving champion and the inventor of modern spring board technique. He attracted a large crowd of spectators who enjoyed the finest display of both springboard and high diving ever seen in the West (Fig. 1.23). One of the spectators at this gala was Ruth Gardiner (cp Fig. 4.14 in Chapter 4) who, in due course, married Vic Moreton. Vic later served as club super-intendent for three years after he retired. Ruth, who is still a club member at the time of writing, shares with Gordon Leyland, another old member, one of the longest memories amongst our current membership; both have been generous in passing their recollections to the authors.

A film was taken at the very special Desjardins gala by the photographer O.W. Dunscombe and presented to the club. In 1998 this film was rescued by the authors, together with many of the archival photographs, from a very damp cardboard box and made into a video. During this memorable year of 1935 A. E. Pearman (a member of Henleaze Swimming Club) set new records in the West for the 100 yards, 220 yards, and 440 yards free style.

In 1936 'Pete' Desjardins returned to take part in another very successful gala at the lake – one of three held during the season – and repeated the diving demonstration he gave in 1935. Henleaze Swimming Club again achieved many successes. Also in that year, the trustees were able to purchase, with money wholly provided by the committee and members of Henleaze Swimming Club, the various parcels of land to

Fig. 1.24 Champion diver Harold 'Dutch' Smith gave a diving display at Henleaze Lake in 1937. Reading the club records, one senses a crescendo of club activity that, in the very near future, the war was to extinguish. (photo Fred Allard)

Fig. 1.25 The Henleaze Ladies Diving Team in one of the last years before World War Two. This charming line-up of highly skilled divers must have attracted a chorus of wolf whistles, a cheerfully tolerated form of unabashed flattery in those carefree days. Diving teams regularly competed in Gloucester County and Western Counties championship events, often achieving notable successes. (photo Anne Floyd née Prater)

secure the entrance to Lake Road at the southeast corner of the lake property. In 1937 another champion diver Harold 'Dutch' Smith gave a highly skilled demonstration of diving at the lake (Fig. 1.24). In 1938 the club was represented in a national championship for the first time for many years when Dorothy Williams competed in the ladies high diving championship at Wembly.

Diving had always been a feature of club life at Henleaze Lake in the two decades before World War Two and then again after the war. Springboard and platform divers were trained by the club's Hon. Diving Coach and notable successes were achieved at championship events. Fig. 1.25 is a photograph of the Ladies Diving Team taken just before the war. Dorothy Williams, centre, held the Western Counties and Gloucester County high board and springboard championships. She was also the first winner of the club's J.A. Bobbett Ladies Diving Trophy in 1938.

The property was constantly being improved in the years leading up to World War Two; more lawns were laid, ground was levelled for car parking, the gents' dressing quarters were established, sanitary arrangements to satisfy health authorities were installed and a starting board was introduced. A poignant letter received in 1995 from Dot Ridley née Brown (reproduced in Chapter 4, Fig. 4.12) states that she and her sister spent all their spare time every summer at the lake from 1925–38 and she often wonders how many of the young dare-devils who used to dive, jump, and even ride their bicycles (with cork floats) off the 10 metre platform, survived to see the end of the war. In the 1930s it was common for groups of teenagers to spend days on end at the lake having what they fondly recalled (and some now still recall) as the time of their lives during the endless hot sunny days.

And so, as the author and broadcaster Helen Dunmore writes in *At The Lake*:

The Lake is full of ghosts, half-hidden in the shadow of the willows or walking out in the mid-day sun. The men wear striped one-piece bathing suits, and stride confidently, masculinely, to the edge of the boards. Their hair is slicked back. They look like Scott Fitzgerald on a good day. They swing their arms back, poise, dive into the sparkling water, and disappear. Even if you rub your eyes you won't see them break the surface again. Women in modest bathing-dresses and rubber bathing-caps duck into the changing-rooms, where the shadows swallow them up. If they saw you, they wouldn't believe in you. They believe in their own perfect day, the present in which they are living, before Hitler and Hiroshima. Their bicycles are flung down on the grass, unchained, and when the closing bell rings they'll cycle off up the white, dusty road which won't be tarmaced for years to come. They are here always, even though they scattered and went to war long ago.

The Club Trophies

A total of 16 magnificent silver cups and bowls have been presented to Henleaze Swimming Club, 11 before the war and five after hostilities ceased. These trophies were valued at £1000 in 1970 and in 2000 they were insured for £8442. The championship trophies are shown in Colour Fig. 1.4; they were mainly donated in memory of early club pioneers and were won each year by club divers and swimmers up to the year 2000, after which their award ceased in acknowledgement of changing times. Each trophy has a plinth on which are engraved the names of scores of champions – some even have double plinths in order to accommodate all the winners' names.

The club's Competition Section turned into the Indoor Section and it finally became a separate club called Bristol Henleaze Swimming Club on 1 January 1993, as will be described in Chapter 2. It takes credit for teaching innumerable children to swim and producing generations of champion divers and swimmers. Now, as a sister club to Henleaze Swimming Club, it continues to be as active as ever, meeting at Bristol North Baths (until they closed in 2005) with occasional use of Henleaze

Lake. Regrettably diving, which was such a strong club feature in the pre-war years, is no longer pursued at competition level.

Below is a list of the championship trophies owned by Henleaze Swimming Club, with the year in which each was presented and the competition in which it was fought for.

1920   The W.J. Taylor cup was presented by Mr Taylor in memory of his son, an active member, whose tragic death occurred at Bristol North Baths during a club training session. The $5^1/2$" wide cup with lid was awarded to the men's 100 yds freestyle champion.

1922   The Stanley H. Badock Cup was presented by Major Badock for an annual life-saving contest to emphasise his concerns for safety. It was awarded in alternate years to men and to women. The last recorded winner of the contest is Miss W. Jones in 1936. The 4" wide cup was subsequently awarded for various competitions, sometimes with a different donor's name, Major Badock having omitted his name from the cup engraving. (This has now been made good.)

The *Bristol Times and Mirror* cup, which was originally a diving trophy, was won outright three times by a club member who then presented it to the club for annual competition. Fig. 1.26 shows several winners of this cup photographed in 1951. From 1969 the 6" wide cup was awarded to the winner of the ladies' 200 yds individual medley.

1923   The Horace Walker cup was donated by Mr H. Walker, a founder member and president of the club. The 5" wide cup was awarded annually to the ladies' freestyle champion over 50 yds, increased to 100 yds in 1927, presumably as the ladies gained stamina.

1928   The William Scantlebury cup was donated by Mr Scantlebury, an active founder club member, president, and first trustee. The 6" wide cup was competed for over 50 yds by boys aged 12 and under.

1931   The Frederick A. Clark memorial rose bowl was donated by Mrs Clark in memory of her husband who lost his life as a result of the Charfield railway disaster near Bristol. The 10" wide bowl was awarded annually to the winner of the men's 220 yds freestyle competition.

1935   The Cecil F. Clark Jubilee cup was presented to the club by Mr Frederick A. Clark's son Mr Cecil F. Clark, a founder member of the club, president, competition secretary, club captain for 29 years, and president of the Amateur Swimming Association in 1959. The 4" wide cup was competed for over 50 yds by girls aged 12 and under.

Fig. 1.26 *The Bristol Times and Mirror Cup* was presented to Henleaze Swimming Club in 1922 as a diving trophy. Our photograph, which was taken in 1951, shows five proud winners of the cup. (Doug Satherley collection)

1936   The W.G. Cox memorial cup was donated by Mrs Cox in memory of her husband Mr W.G. Cox, a founder member of the club. The 4" wide cup with lid was awarded to the winner of the men's 100 yds back stroke competition.

1938   The James A. Bobbett cup was donated by Mr James A. Bobbett as a ladies' diving trophy. He was a club trustee, president and active member, known especially for his early morning swims. The $5^1/2$" cup was later applied to other events.

The G.M. Bobbett cup was presented by Mrs Bobbett in memory of her husband Mr James A. Bobbett as a men's diving trophy. This was amended in 1969 to the men's 100 yds breast stroke competition. The cup is 7" wide.

The Malaya trophy (a silver bowl) was presented by Mr D.A. Stephen to commemorate the demolition of the old lime kiln. Mr Stephen was a very active and popular member in the early days of the club. He served in Malaya during the war and left Bristol for an appointment in the Far East. The 8" wide bowl was originally awarded to the winner of the men's fancy diving championship, but amended in 1969 to the men's 200 yds individual medley.

1948   The Ethel M. Cartridge cup was presented by Miss 'Bunty' Cartridge in memory of her parents (Ethel is her mother) who had both been keen supporters of the club. Miss Cartridge swam for the club on numerous occasions and won Bristol, Gloucester and Western Counties events. The 4^1/$_2$" wide cup was for 'Triers', being awarded to try-hards with acclaim. Sadly, Bunty Cartridge lost two brothers and her boyfriend in World War Two.

1950   The S.W. Robinson cup was donated by Miss Robinson in memory of her father Mr S.W. Robinson, a former president and committee member, for the ladies' 100 yds breast stroke competition. The cup is 3" wide.

1957   The J. McCullock cup was presented by the McCullock family on the death of Mr McCullock, who was the competition secretary for many years. The 4" wide cup was awarded to the ladies' 220 yds freestyle winner.

1969   The Skeeby cup was presented by Mr Skeeby in appreciation of the club's efforts in training his granddaughter to achieve a very high standard in swimming. The 2^1/$_2$" wide cup, which has been listed in error as the Keeby cup a number of times, was awarded to the winner of the 100 yds breast stroke competition for girls aged 12 and under.

1982   The George Derrick memorial cup was donated by Mrs Derrick in memory of her husband Mr Derrick who was strongly associated with the club's competitive section. The 2" cup was given for the 100 yds breast stroke competition for boys aged 12 and under.

A list of championship trophies and the names on the plinths reveals how club involvement was frequently a family matter with relationships between donors, and between donors and champions. Superintendents were sometimes a part of the family too, a tradition that can be traced to this day. As an illustration we reproduce, by kind permission of their daughter Janet Cocks (cp next section) a photograph of Archie Macfarlane club superintendent and Blanche 'Bunny' Clark after their marriage taken outside St Albans church in Westbury Park in 1927 (Fig. 1.27). Miss Clark, a club swimming champion, is the daughter of Frederick A. Clark (the donor of a cup above) and the sister of Cecil F. Clark (also the donor of a cup above) and Charles E. Clark, a club water polo captain.

Fig. 1.27 Bon Voyage! Miss Blanche Clark, a 50 yards ladies' championship holder of Henleaze Swimming Club is married to Mr Archie Macfarlane, club superintendent, at St Albans Church, Westbury Park on 5 November 1927. Miss Clark is the daughter of cup donor Frederick Clark and the sister of cup donor Cecil Clark. Archie Macfarlane was elected club president in 1958. (photo Janet Cocks née Macfarlane)

VETERAN SKY-DIVER DIES ON MOUNTAIN WALK

2x Henleaze Club members

Farewell

Sometime HSC superintendant and President 1958.

to brave

Archie

Bristol Evening Post, Wednesday, September 23, 1987

By Ben Preston

SKY-DIVING pensioner Archie MacFarlane has been found dead in his beloved Welsh mountains.

Mr MacFarlane, of High Grove, Sea Mills, Bristol, who sky-dived into the record books at the age of 89, was found lying in a mountain stream by an RAF search party.

Rescue teams and a helicopter from Valley RAF station, Anglesey, had mounted a search after Archie disappeared in the desolate Arran Mountains, Gwynedd.

Record

He had gone out for a walk on Monday but failed to return to the farmhouse where he was staying near Dinas Mawddy.

The slight widower is listed in the Guinness Book of Records as the oldest fall-guy. He leaped to fame in May when he became the oldest parachutist in the world to freefall tandem.

A Somme veteran, Mr MacFarlane took up parachuting at the age of 75 after telling instructors he was only 60.

He entered the record books with a jump from 10,000 feet.

That achievement earned him an Order of Merit from the Royal Aeroclub — and a personal presentation by the Duke of York.

He said his one regret was that he had to make the jump strapped to his instructor.

Walking

"They wouldn't let me do it on my own even though I wanted to," he said. "We are all a bit soft in this country."

For Archie, life took on a new meaning at 65, as he tried swimming, rock climbing, tobogganning, fell

walking and travelling the world.

As a pensioner Archie sold his 350cc motorcycle to pay for a South African safari, and sold his television and video to finance a day trip to Iceland on Concorde. To make the trip more exciting he took a domestic flight from Reykjavik to a neighbouring island.

Archie had loved walking in the Arran Mountains for a quarter of a century, and was known there as the "King of the Mountains".

Mr Idwal Jones, aged 73, at whose farmhouse he had been staying, said he had been anxious about how far Mr MacFarlane intended to walk on Monday. He had looked more frail than usual.

Mr Jones added: "He would have been 90 in January. I knew he would not survive a

night on the mountains because the weather was so severe.

"We tried to persuade him not to go too far."

Archie's daughter, Janet, who lives in Bristol, planned to visit the scene of his death today.

Archie was a regular at the Progress Inn, Sea Mills, where he used to drink brown splits with his former son-in-law

Lord Cocks of Hartcliffe.

Friend of 50 years Mr Don Egland, of Sea Mills, said Archie was a popular figure in the area.

"Everybody knew him and said hello to him. He was a very active bloke who used to go tobogganing on Shirehampton Golf Course up until recently," he said.

Archie was recently

chosen to head British Rail's promotion of senior citizen railcards in the "Experience of a Lifetime" competition.

"He was chosen because Archie had done everything which other people wrote to us saying they would like to do," said spokesman Mr Alan Harrison.

"He was a people person who thrived on any social atmosphere," he said.

Archie MacFarlane, pictured just before his parachute jump

Fig. 1.28 Farewell to brave Archie Macfarlane, sometime swimming club superintendent and president, who married a club champion. This clipping from the *Bristol Evening Post* tells us about Archie who is one of the club's colourful erstwhile worthies. (kindly supplied by Ruth Moreton)

Archie Macfarlane was elected club president in 1958 (superintendents have become presidents three times in the club's history), being one of the six years that his older brother Regie Macfarlane was chairman of the executive committee. A number of club pioneers have been identified in the background of this splendid picture. Archie Macfarlane entered the *Guinness Book of Records* in 1987 as the oldest tandem parachutist at the age of 89 (Fig. 1.28). He made his first parachute jump at the age of 75 after telling his instructor he was only 60.

Looking Back

Writing in July 2005, Janet Cocks née Macfarlane (cp previous section) has given us her personal reminiscences of the pre-war years at Henleaze Lake:

I was first introduced to 'The Lake' over seventy years ago. My father, Archie Macfarlane was the Superintendent at the time and my mother, brother and I used to accompany him to the lake every day during the summer months. My parents were founder members of Henleaze Swimming Club at its inception in 1919, long before my brother and I were born of course. My parents met at the lake after Dad returned from the First World War. They met again when Dad came back from Australia where he had gone looking for work during the depression. They were married in 1927 and there is a very nice photo of them [Fig. 1.27] on display in the little room at the lake where you can nowadays make tea. Dad was the Club's Superintendent for four years and then went to work for BAC (The Bristol Aeroplane Company Ltd) at Filton.

My parents were enthusiastic swimmers, though Mum was probably the stronger of the two. I still have a collection of Mum's swimming medals and a replica of the Horace Walker Cup that she won in 1923 for the Ladies 50 yards Club Championship. I have also a vast collection of old black and white photos, some of which have been copied and are on display with the wedding photo I mentioned.

As we grew the lake was the main place where we spent our spare time; being there became a big part of my life. Regardless of the weather we were there. I recall wet days, cold days, but we still managed to swim all through the Season. Maybe there was very little else to occupy our time then, but I remember being very happy. I even recall one very cold winter when the lake froze over. I was able to borrow some skates and somehow managed to stay upright for some of the time. I doubt if we would be allowed to do this in these days of Health and Safety!

On Friday nights my brother and I attended the Learners Section of the Club at Bristol North Baths. I struggled to swim and remember on one occasion being attached to a sort of harness around my waist which was attached to a rope. I was then made to swim from the deep end by my uncle, Cecil Clark (former President of Henleaze Swimming Club). Needless to say I sank, much to his amusement and I was put off swimming for some time! The Second World War came shortly after and the baths were closed. I think they must have opened again shortly after, because I finally was eligible to become a Club member in about 1943 after proving that I could swim 50 yards. I think that even my parents were surprised that at last I could swim. Incidentally my cousins who lived nearby in Hill Grove, Henleaze during the war recall being driven to the lake during air raids in order to shelter in the cave which still exists at the right of the entrance as you come in.

I also remember that there were regular Galas that took place each summer. I was an indifferent swimmer but was entered for a few breaststroke events. I was never as good as my mother who was the Breaststroke Queen! Fig. 1.29 is probably a press photo of those who were present at a Club Gala held in 1920 or 1921. Press reporters were invariably present. Many of the 62 people in this old photograph are founding officers and members of Henleaze Swimming Club. Others appear to be from a visiting club. There were often

Fig. 1.29 This photograph is dated at 1920 or 1921. It is probably a press photo taken at a Club Gala and it shows many of the club's founding officers and members. Janet Cocks' mother-to-be Blanche 'Bunny' Clark aged 18 or 19 sits on the diving board directly below the horn. Janet's father-to-be Archie Macfarlane is to the left of the end of the diving board holding his younger sister, and Janet's grandmother Constance Clark is third in from the right, second row down, in a broad brimmed hat and dark skirt. Her grandfather Frederick Clark does not appear to be present. Founding officers Cecil Clark (Janet's Uncle), Regie Macfarlane (Archie's brother), G.H. Chivers, and Reg Kidd are all present. The photograph, which is taken against the quarry cliff wall between the diving tower and the ladies' changing tent, shows the water edge before the bank was built up. (photo Janet Cocks née Macfarlane)

brass bands at these early Galas which could account for the horn. Water Polo was also a strong feature of life at the lake. Every weekend there seem to have been Water Polo Matches which were well supported. I was a bit of a Water Polo 'Groupie' following the team to Cheltenham, Gloucester, Portland and the rest. Oh happy days!

I gave up my membership shortly after I got married and family and other commitments took over. In 2002 my membership was renewed by two friends as a surprise special birthday present. After over 40 years I am a member again and it has been a truly memorable experience. There have been some changes of course but the lake is still the same magic place to me as it was all those years ago.

The diving stage has been reduced in height but is as popular as ever. The disappearance of the practice diving board over the sandpit is a notable loss to would be divers and small children alike. The installation of the ladies' shower is a real luxury, though the vague damp smell in the ladies' changing rooms brings back real memories. I wonder if the matting there is the same? I think not. The men's changing rooms seem to be the same, though they are not usually visited by me I hasten to add! The grounds are so very well maintained and there are flowers everywhere that I do not recall in the past. Are the willow trees still the same ones I wonder? The water still seems cold to me and not so inviting as it was when I was young, but I intend to continue my membership for a few years yet. It's good to be back.

CHAPTER 2
THE WAR AND AFTER

Time, you thief, who love to get,
Sweets in your list, put that in!
Leigh Hunt

The War

Although Henleaze Swimming Club continued to function during the war, there was little activity at the lake beyond the purely recreational and there was no Annual General Meeting for the seven years 1939 to 1945. Uniformed members of H.M. Forces were admitted to the lake for 6d. Only a couple of rather basic membership cards from this period have survived. The number of club members during this period averaged 487 with a peak of 543 in 1942. These figures include the many honorary memberships that were issued to armed forces service men and women who were able to enjoy the lake during the war, either whilst on leave or whilst stationed in the area. As well as our own servicemen and women, it was not unusual to see American, Canadian, and even French soldiers for whom there was a special forces membership category at the lake (Fig. 2.1).

Fig. 2.1 A group photograph, dated May 1944, taken at the lake towards the end of the war when American soldiers were billeted in private homes in the district surrounding the lake. The Americans would sometimes be seen at the lake during their off-duty periods. (photo Jill Chaffey)

Following the outbreak of hostilities in 1939 the Trustees and Executive Committee resolved that the club would carry on as long as circumstances permitted. They also resolved to suspend the application of any club rule other than those relating to safety measures. Throughout the war years regular laboratory tests of the lake water were made. These tests proved the water to be in exceptionally good condition and safe and suitable for bathing. Some of the facilities afforded by the club to meet the changed conditions occasioned by the war were formally documented as follows:

1. Throughout the war years honorary membership was granted to all paid up members of the club while they were serving with H.M. Forces and the Nursing Services, and facilities were also extended to individual members of H.M. Forces who were not members to swim in the lake at a reduced entrance fee, provided they complied with certain conditions laid down by the club.
2. Henleaze was able to assist other swimming clubs, most of whose members were evacuated, to keep together and carry on their activities whilst residing in Bristol.
3. Several military units stationed in the vicinity were granted special permission to bring parties to the lake from time to time and one or two units in the immediate neighbourhood sent regular parties under a competent N.C.O.
4. The National Fire Services were granted permission to use the lake at stated times for hose drill, and they subsequently laid a pipe line to the water's edge for relaying water should the necessity arise.
5. It may be remembered that in the early days of the war a V.A.D. Hospital was opened in St. Peter's Hall and permits were issued to the convalescing soldiers there to visit the lake as spectators. Members of the club provided the necessary transport for these parties.
6. Early in 1942 the club committee decided to send a monthly parcel of cigarettes to members who were known to be prisoners of war, and this continued until these members were repatriated.

The club's Diving Section had many successes in 1939 and 1940 in local and county events but after 1940 no further diving championships were held until after the war. There were also neither water polo trials nor tournaments during the war but polo was the first sport to be resumed in 1946 with seniors training for the 1948 Olympic Games. The Learners Section (forerunner of the Indoor Section) reformed in October 1945. Prior to the war this section had functioned at Bristol North Baths during the summer months only but the section's activities were now extended to the winter months.

The lake property did not emerge untouched from the German blitz. On 25 September 1940 at 11.48 a.m. 57 Heinkel III aircraft made one pass over the Filton aircraft works of the Bristol Aeroplane Company (BAC), dropping 100 tons of bombs in 15 seconds. This disastrous air raid, which caused extensive damage and loss of life, is described in detail in Kenneth Wakefield's book *Target Filton*. A commemorative service was held at Filton House, the headquarters of BAC, on the 50th anniversary of the daylight raid in 1990 and there is a memorial plaque recording the names of the victims in Filton Parish Church. A stray stick of bombs fell into Southmead and Henleaze. There was considerable bomb damage in Lake Road adjacent to Henleaze Lake, where the houses numbers 45 and 47 adjoining the lake were flattened and several other houses were so extensively damaged that the residents had to leave. One of the bombs did not explode and was not accounted for. It is alleged by an eye witness to have fallen into the water at the northern end of Henleaze Lake and may well still lie there under the mud to this day.

The war ends

At the end of the war in 1945 the lake property was very neglected, and it was necessary to spend a lot of money on repairs and equipment. Subscription rates were raised and activities presently recommenced in force. Water polo was played again (Fig. 2.2); in July 1946 the English Inter-District Water Polo Tournament was held at the lake, the first occasion that teams representing the North, Northeast, Midlands, South, and West Districts had been brought together at one venue. The President of the ASA and members of the English Water Polo Selection Committee were present. These galas and tournaments were huge events, were advertised extensively and required an enormous amount of organisation, which was all done by volunteers.

Fig. 2.2 Water polo matches were popular spectator events in the post-war years, with large numbers of the public watching, especially when star players like Weston-super-mare's formidable Dave Hambro was playing against Henleaze. The lake attracted teams from all over Great Britain and even some from abroad. This picture was taken at Henleaze Lake in the late 1950s. (photo Fred Allard)

In August 1947 the leading British water polo players and high divers attended a training week at the lake, which culminated with teams representing Great Britain competing against Sweden in water polo and diving. Fig. 2.3 shows the relevant pages from the Club Gala programme for 9 August 1947 at which these events, amongst others, were staged. A flag pole was set up at the entrance to Henleaze Lake (the plinth is still there, see Fig. 2.4) so that visiting teams could display their flags in addition to the Union Jack and/or the Henleaze flag.

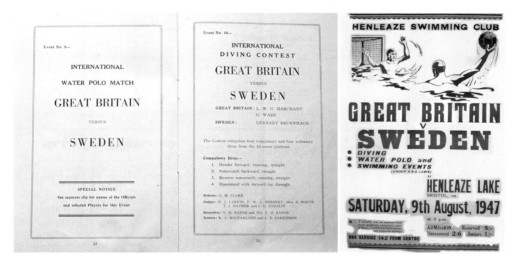

Fig. 2.3 Two pages from the 20-page Club Gala programme (price 6d) and the poster for Saturday 9 August 1947. International competitive events were often a feature of life at the lake in the post-war years. In this particular polo match Great Britain was thrashed by 9 goals to 1.

A high level of competitive enthusiasm was indeed pursued at the lake in those days. The polo referees enjoyed a built-up rock walkway that enabled them to walk up and down the length of the polo pitch on the east (Lake Road) side as well as the landed west side. We have mentioned in Chapter 1 that the remains of this walkway still exist (cp Fig.1.9). On the other (Lakewood Road) side of the pitch the referees had a leaning bar which is still there. No doubt this enabled the referee to stand his ground safely away from the water in times of excitement.

In the late 1940s Olympic trials and training were held at Henleaze Lake, reaching a crescendo in 1947, the year before the Olympic Games in London. Amongst the club's guests were some of Great Britain's biggest Olympic hopes. During the trials Johnny Weissmüller, the film star who played Tarzan in twelve Hollywood Tarzan films (notably the 1932 film *The Ape Man* in which he starred with Maureen O'Sullivan) gave a demonstration of swimming and diving. It was not unusual for crowds to watch such events from the east cliff top (Lake Road side), there being access all along the length of the cliff top providing a grandstand view of the activities. Spectators would also swarm up the cliffs on the west (Lakewood Road side). As a thank you to Henleaze Swimming Club for the use of their facilities for training, the Canadian Olympic team staged a diving display at the lake in 1948.

Fig. 2.4 The old flag pole plinth at the entrance to Henleaze Lake. Doug Satherley, war-time rear gunner in a bomber and the club's Hon. Diving Coach, created the plinth and left his mark on the back. In its heyday the blue and yellow Henleaze club flag would flutter from the flag pole together with the Union Jack or a visiting club's flag. (photo Mark Thompson)

One of the memorable acts involved a character dressed up as Hitler giving the heil salute goose-stepping off the 10 metre platform.

David Prowse was another character at the lake who went on to Hollywood stardom – as Darth Vader in *Star Wars*. He was the club's superintendent in 1960 and 1961 and also a competitive body builder who trained hard and became the author of several books on the subject. All who met him were impressed with his exceptional physical dimensions. The records state that he was 6 feet 7 inches tall – quite enough to attract a bevy of adoring girls whilst weightlifting at the lake (Fig. 2.5) and, of course, to deter any misbehaviour amongst the boys and girls. The superintendent Sergeant Fred Beaumont (ex-police) was another person who kept impeccable order at the lake during this period. He lived in Lakewood Road and his garden commanded a full view of what was going on down below at the lake. A shout from the sergeant would put off any potential delinquent.

Fig. 2.5 Dave Prowse was the superintendent at Henleaze Lake in 1960 and 1961. He was a competitive body builder who trained hard, often at the lake before admiring onlookers. His books on the subject describe training techniques for all wannabees. He went on to Hollywood stardom as Darth Vader in *Star Wars* and was also the Green Cross Man who took children safely across the road in a government campaign on road safety in the 1970s. In 2000 Dave was awarded the MBE in the Millennium Honours List. In June 2005 Dave attended the club's Midsummer Party and presented the awards for the plunging competition. (photos David Prowse)

The Lake Cliff Top Property

In 1999 the Land Registry completed the registration of the club's title no. BL60682 to its land and issued the Land Registry Plan shown in Fig. 2.6. This plan clearly sets out the boundaries of the land bought by Henleaze Swimming Club in 1933. The club owns the cliff top land on the east for a varying distance of up to three or four metres back from the cliff edge. There was formerly a footpath which ran between the club's cliff top land and the ends of the back gardens of Lake Road residents (Fig. 2.7).

For many years the club maintained a fence that ran along the boundary between the footpath and club land. This fence was continually being broken down and in the years since the club was founded two persons who had breached the fence fell from the cliff top into the deep water and drowned. There was very nearly a third fatality in 1928, the victim only being saved in a dramatic rescue. A contemporary account of the rescue is given in Fig. 1.20 in Chapter 1. The account illustrates how steep high cliffs on the east side of the lake plunge into deep water.

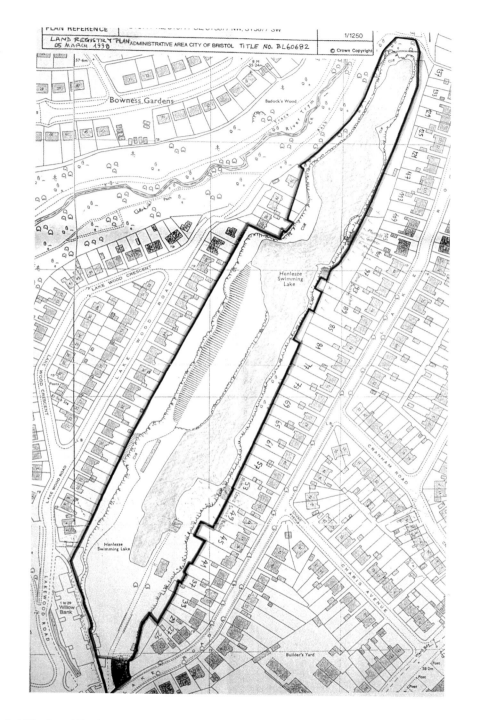

Fig. 2.6 The Land Registry Plan issued with Henleaze Swimming Club's title no. BL60682. The club bought the land in 1933 and registration was completed in 1999. The club owns a strip of land of variable width back from the cliff edge on both the east and west cliff tops. (plan by Land Registry)

40

HENLEAZE LAKE FOOTPATH DANGER

Fig. 2.7 This photograph shows the footpath along the top of the cliffs on the east side of the lake as it was in June 1939. The footpath ran between the club's cliff top land and the back gardens of Lake Road residents. Judging by the proximity of the cliff edge shown in this press photograph, the path must have passed quite close to the cliff edge in places. Despite continual maintenance of its boundary fences by the club, there were calls to close the path on the grounds of safety. The right of way was finally withdrawn in 1940 and the land on which the footpath ran was ceded to Lake Road residents after the war. (*Western Daily Press and Bristol Mirror*, 24 June 1939)

As a result, both the swimming club and the City Council became keen for the path to be closed and in 1939 the Bristol Juvenile Organisation Committee added its voice to a campaign, in order 'to safeguard children who may stray into this danger spot'. Evidently a child protection agency was in existence even before the war. A desire to close off the footpath was also expressed by Lake Road residents because during the war the blackout made it easy for burglars to penetrate the back gardens of the houses.

After an altercation with The Ramblers Association, the provision of access to allotments rented on club land, and a lengthy, costly (of course) legal procedure, the right of way along the footpath was withdrawn in 1940. However it was still possible to use the footpath. As late as 1947 large pieces of rock were still being dislodged by vandals and tipped into the lake. In that year Laurie McGowan, the swimming club's long-serving Hon. Secretary appealed to the City Council for help (Fig. 2.8). The City Engineer's response was to erect a triple coil barbed wire fence.

In 1948 the land on which the 4ft wide footpath ran was finally ceded to the Lake Road residents by the City Council, enabling residents to fence it off. Even so, one can still see in some places the posts which betray where the footpath once

HENLEAZE SWIMMING CLUB

President—R. A. MACFARLANE

Hon. Treasurer—
A. E. PARKINSON
60 Arbutus Drive, Coombe Dingle
Tel. Bristol 82690

Hon. Secretary—
L. A. McGOWAN
35 Upper Cranbrook Road, Redland
Bristol, 6
Tel. Bristol 44179

Affiliated to—
Western Counties Amateur Swimming Association.   Gloucester County Amateur Swimming Association
Royal Life Saving Society

Lake Tel. No. 662791

BRISTOL 19th August, 1947.

The City Engineer,
    Corporation of Bristol,
        7, College Fields,
            Bristol, 8.

Dear Sir,
                    It was recently reported to me
by the owner of some land on the Lake Road side
(Southmead end) of our property that some of the
older lads in the neighbourhood were dislodging
large pieces of rock and tipping them into the
Lake. On inspection I found that a considerable
quantity of rock had thus been forcibly removed
and unfortunately this is still going on.

                    Large numbers of young children as
well as the rougher element make this end of the
Lake their playground, and although the Police
have been informed, we have the co-operation of
nearby residents, and we ourselves are constantly
turning these trespassers away, we fail to stop
them completely. The young children clamber down
the rock face, which in itself is a source of danger,
but with falling rock it is doubly so, and sooner
or later a very serious accident is likely to occur.

                    The fencing which you had erected
some time ago has been deliberately cut in many
places and does not seem to be effective in
preventing the children and others from approaching
what is a very dangerous spot.

Fig. 2.8 The fence on the club's cliff-top boundary on the east, Lake Road, side of the lake was continually being broken down before, during and after the World War Two. The damage enabled children to access the dangerous cliff edge and vandals to dislodge rocks. This letter was written in 1947 by the swimming club's Hon. Secretary Laurie McGowan to ask the City Engineer for help with the serious safety and security problem. The City Engineer responded by providing more substantial barbed wire fencing.

Colour Fig. P.1 View of Henleaze Lake taken from a hot air balloon in 1996.
(photo Capt. David Thornley)

Colour Fig. 1.1 Portrait of Sir Stanley Hugh Badock 1867–1945. Stanley Badock, who lived at Holmwood in Westbury-on-Trym (now Holmwood House Nursing Home) was instrumental to the founding of Henleaze Swimming Club. A staunch friend and patron of the club until his death, he was its early helmsman, benefactor and a club Vice-President. (with permission University of Bristol)

Colour Fig. 1.2 The remains of a wall built in 1934, when the water in the lake largely disappeared, to keep mud back from the diving area. This photograph was taken in October 1988 when the lake water level was pumped down to enable Wessex Water Authority (as it was then) to make a detailed fishing survey. Stocks of many different varieties of fish have subsequently been built up by the bailiffs using the survey information. (photo Derek Klemperer)

Colour Fig. 1.3 Clare Meehan and Carol Holloway, both long serving club trustees, in 2006. Clare models the club blazer which was often worn at club galas and dances both before and after World War Two. Carol née Good, who was Club Captain in the 1970s, holder of various Club Championships, and Hon. Club Secretary for 17 years until 2005 holds a replica of the club crest. (photo Mark Thompson)

Colour Fig. 1.4 These 16 Championship Cups were given to the club from the earliest years. Each cup has a plinth or plinths on which the names of club champions down through the years are engraved. The cups were presented to club champions for the last time in 2000. (photo Mark Thompson)

Colour Fig. 2.1 Yellow irises growing on the waters edge at Henleaze Lake. These water plants do not stand drying out and have to be reintroduced after the water level recovers following a drought. (photo Mervyn Rowles)

Colour Fig. 2.2 *Left:* The floating pontoon which was installed in May 2003. The pontoon replaced the starting board structure that had to be winched up and down on sloping rails to accommodate water level changes. The new installation, which floats up and down with the variations in water level, presents a constant height above the water level for swimmers and divers alike. Access to the pontoon is via a hinged ramp. Bob Teesdale (pictured) was the first one to try it out. (photo Ross Harley) *Right:* The pontoon shown being put in place by a crane. The design, construction, and installation of the entire structure was undertaken by Intermarine Ltd., liaising with the club's Ross Harley. (photo Derek Klemperer)

Colour Fig. 3.1 This photograph shows lake bank where three concrete swims (places to fish from) are hidden by phragmites and other natural plant growth. Concrete swims are popular and maintenance-free and cannot be seen from the water. (photo Joyce Klemperer)

Colour Fig.3.2 A junior fishing member proudly displays the first tench he caught in Henleaze Lake. This photograph won the 1st prize in the swimming club's 80th birthday photographic competition in 1999. (photo Lee Hannan)

Colour Fig. 3.3 An angler 'bivvied up' for night fishing at the lake. (photo Gary Bray)

Colour Fig. 3.4 A 5 lbs bream caught in Henleaze Lake in 2006. Bream are characteristically thin fish with low-slung bodies. (photo Duance Lee)

Colour Fig. 3.5 An angler 'playing' a carp. (photo Gary Bray)

Colour Fig. 3.6 An 18 lbs common carp caught from a swim on the board walks at Henleaze Lake. The lake contains a variety of carp over 10 lbs in weight, against which carp anglers can match their wits. (photo Colin Hannan)

Fig. 2.9 Old fence posts photographed in the back garden of number 43 Lake Road in April 2002 reveal where the former footpath ran close to the cliff top above Henleaze Lake. The footpath, which was closed during the war, was ceded to Lake Road residents in 1948. Henleaze Swimming Club owns the cliff top land which lies between the cliff edge and the boundary of the former footpath; this land is 3 or 4 metres wide. Until 1968 the club officers would walk right round the lake at cliff top level at least once a year 'beating the bounds'. (photo Derek Klemperer)

ran (Fig. 2.9) and there is still a stone wall along parts of the old path boundary at its northern reaches. One of the older Lake Road residents remembers that it was once so wide that a pony trap would pass by on the land between the back of his garden and the cliff top and cyclists regularly used this route. Older club members remember the path well. For some it was the first sight of the lake and the discovery of the lake's existence; others recall repartee between those on the cliff top and sunbathers below.

In 1963 the Bristol Rediffusion Service extended a cable into the club's cliff top land at the rear of Lake Road gardens. An annual rent was paid to the club 'for as long as the works remain on the property'. Although rent has not been paid for decades, the defunct cable is still there and Lake Road residents sometimes strike it with a shovel when they extend their gardens onto lake property.

The club also owns a much wider strip of cliff top land on the east, i.e. Lakewood Road side of the lake. Until 1968 club officers would beat the bounds at least once a year before the swimming season opened by walking right around the club boundary at cliff top level. There are stories of how the club's Wing Commander R.A. Belcher, who died in 1957 whilst serving as president, would stand no nonsense from obstructers during this exercise. After 1968 beating the bounds ceased due, as Fred Allard has written, 'to sheer slackness'. We may see here the gradual beginnings of the slide towards a period of recession for the club which took hold in subsequent decades before the club eventually regained its enthusiasm in more recent times.

Both the northern and southern ends of club land on the Lake Road cliff top appear to have been sealed off some time after 1968. In the north D.J. Venn summarily constructed a sturdy brick wall ostensibly to protect the goats and chickens he kept up there from passing people – the chicken sheds still exist (Fig. 2.10). In a letter dated 1 February 1976 to the swimming club's Hon. Secretary, D.J. Venn contests that 'the piece of land adjoining Henleaze Lake which I use . . . is the property of Henleaze Swimming Club' adding 'I do not intend to suffer this any longer' and 'I do not want anybody snooping about on my land'. The 'Venn wall' is very easy to see from Badock Woods where the passage from Lake Road reaches the woods. In the south, 25 Lake Road extended its garden to the cliff edge and fenced it in (the extension is now legally owned by number 25). One can still see where the cliff top access once emerged onto Lake Road.

These barriers completely isolated the club land between the cliff edge and the end of the Lake Road residents' gardens, most of it lying directly above the water. By the late 1970s D.J. Venn had acquired a strip of club land by adverse possession

Fig. 2.10 Sheds believed to be those in which D.J. Venn kept his chickens still exist beyond the gardens of Lake Road residents. This photograph, taken in July 2004, shows the sheds beyond the gardens of 105, 107, and 109 Lake Road. The prominent stone wall runs along the border between cliff top land and Lake Road residents' gardens. The wooden fence in the background is just 2 feet from the cliff edge. (photo Andrew Mantell)

(squatters' rights) and offered it for sale to any Lake Road residents who wished to buy it. Meanwhile some gardens were extended to the cliff edge while other pockets of club land became overgrown. This produced today's land patchwork on the east cliff top (Lake Road side). Of the club's 56 pieces of cliff top land abutting Lake Road properties some ten have been lost by adverse possession since 1968. This has occurred quite legally despite the club's robust opposition, English law being what it was until 2005.

Although access to the club's cliff top land is invariably via Lake Road residents' gardens (with their permission), the swimming club regularly maintains its trees on the cliff top. The club now also steadfastly maintains ownership of its cliff top land, as defined in the land registry's title, so that the planning of any permanent buildings can immediately be opposed. This is especially of concern where a building would overlook the lake. The club also requires that no fences are erected to enclose club land. The club must also be able to oppose any pursuit of offensive activities on the cliff top such as pollution / tipping, undermining and destabilising the cliff, wild noisy parties, and the uninhibited growth of noxious or overhanging undergrowth. At the same time the club is perfectly content for Lake Road residents to use club cliff top land for growing fruit, vegetables, flowers, or a lawn should they wish to do so.

On the other hand, the club land on the west cliff top (Lakewood Road side of the lake) is bounded below not by water but almost entirely by the car park, lawns and woods and is therefore quite accessible all along its length. The club officers have always kept control of this land for which peppercorn rents are sought from the Lakewood Road residents who wish to use the land adjoining their gardens for gardening or as allotments. The club boundary was marked by a concrete path, most of which is still in place (Fig. 2.11 left) and one can find the odd surveyor's peg precisely where it was put (Fig. 2.11 right).

Life Saving and Diving

The Royal Life Saving Society held Life Guard Proficiency Test training sessions in the lake during the summer of 1949 and many club members gained awards. Diving became well established in the post war years with many impressive displays. In 1949 and 1950 The Western Counties Amateur Swimming Association staged Diving Training Schools at the lake whilst The National School of Diving with 15 pupils and 7 coaches held a training week at the lake in August 1950. In the same year the old wooden diving structure shown in Figs. 1.21, 1.23, and 2.12, along with the changing room underneath, was demolished and replaced by a new steel Olympic diving tower.

The design and construction of the new steel diving tower was undertaken by The Metal Agencies Co. Ltd. of Bristol working in close conjunction with the club's officers and divers. The diving courses held at the lake honed the skills of coaches as well as pupils (including some of our home grown champions) and undoubtedly gave impetus to the installation of the new tower. Fig. 2.13 shows the steel diving tower being enjoyed on a hot summer's day in 1989. In a sense the pictures of diving

Fig. 2.11 *Left:* A part of the concrete path which runs along the top of the west cliff above the lake defining the boundary of the club's property. This photograph was taken in 1997 looking south. *Right:* One of the original surveyor's pegs still in place defining the club's boundary on the west cliff top (Lakewood Road side). This peg, situated next to a fence post base, is one of several that existed when this photograph was taken in 1997. (photos Derek Klemperer)

towers are timeless because they represent the high diving facilities that were used and enjoyed at the lake by generations of club members and guests to the club.

One of the problems the club has lived with throughout its existence is the way the water level changes. This problem will be discussed in Chapter 3. Even in winter the level can fall well below the flagged edge of the lake but more usually in the past water has had to be pumped out in winter, there being no natural outflow. On the other hand, during the summer months the water level invariably falls by a metre or two. Such water level fluctuations kill pretty well all water plants that grow on the waters edge except glyceria and the voracious phragmites; the popular yellow irises (Colour Fig. 2.1) simply have to be reintroduced after a drought.

Big level falls have in the past necessitated the temporary closure of the 10 metre diving stage and called for a starting board for swimming races that could be lowered and raised to accommodate changes in the water level. Post-war gala pictures of swimming races (Fig. 2.14) show that the starting board then in use could be manhandled up or down a number of steps that had been cast into the concrete wall buttresses at the swimming end of the lake (Fig. 2.15).

Fig. 2.12 48 club members and visitors pose on the wooden diving tower that was erected at Henleaze Lake in the 1920s. This marvellous picture was taken by the *Bristol Evening World* and kindly supplied by Joan Marshman. One of the then young ladies recognised herself in this picture and informed us that it was taken in 1932. The wooden tower was the second to be erected at Henleaze Lake. It boasted a changing room built into the bottom of the structure and also had a space for championship judges to sit and look out through an opening. Note the old lime kiln on the right hand side of the picture. The first diving tower at Henleaze Lake, shown in Figs. 1.16 and 1.17 in Chapter 1, is a far more rudimentary structure.

In 1948 a 'landing bay' was designed with a continuously variable level. A substantial angle-iron frame bearing boards on top was to be raised and lowered using 10 cwt hoists at each end. Although the structure was never completed at the time, the angle iron frame was produced and used in 1957 for an improved starting board system. In the new system shown in Fig. 2.15, the angle iron frame ran up and down on sloping rails. The starting boards were fixed onto the top of the frame and the frame was moved up or down with a single worm operated winch.

With the demise of championship racing events at the lake after 1963, the starting board installation was used purely for recreational diving and some diving classes. The rails were later removed. The original frame was also extended to reach further out over the water to get well away from the old concrete steps below the water. The platforms on the high diving tower were extended in the same way in 2000 to give

Fig. 2.13 Henleaze Swimming Club in high session, July 1989. This photograph shows the steel Olympic diving tower with 5, 7, and 10 metre platforms that was built at the Lake in 1950 to replace the older wooden structure shown in Fig. 2.12. It is the third diving tower to be erected on this site. This picture has been widely reproduced (it appears in three books) and it is the subject of a popular club post card. Three other views of the lake were also produced as post cards in 1996 for sale to club members and their guests. (photo Derek Klemperer)

greater clearance over the submerged rocky bank. Risk assessment is always to the fore nowadays in accordance with Health and Safety legislation.

In 2003 the angle iron frame supporting the starting boards (Fig. 2.15) had become seriously corroded and failed its 'MOT'. It had not been possible to adjust its height to accommodate water level changes for decades so the whole structure was replaced by a pontoon that floats up and down with the lake water level (Colour Fig. 2.2 left). The new one ton structure was positioned in the lake with a crane, as shown in Colour Fig. 2.2 right.

In 1950, the year that the steel diving tower was erected, a high chain link fence with iron entrance gates was also erected on the Lake Road club boundary. The fence was replaced in 2000 but the steel diving structure and the entrance gates have been well maintained and are still in good condition well over half a century later, although sadly, and unnecessarily, the 10 metre diving platform has perforce been taken out of use since 1991 (discussed in Chapter 4).

From 1949–56 the club's Hon. Diving Coach was Doug Satherley. He survived the war, flying 31 ops. as a rear gunner in Lancaster bombers – the life of a rear

Fig. 2.14 The start to a swimming race in about 1950. This photograph shows the starting board then in use which could be heaved up and down the concrete steps to accommodate large changes in water level. Note the swimming club blazers being worn. The blazers are in the club colours of royal blue, light blue, and bright yellow. (photo Fred Allard)

Fig. 2.15 The starting board frame as it was 1957 to 2003. Boards were fixed to the top of the frame which could be winched up or down on sloping rails to accommodate changes in the lake water level. This photo was taken by Derek Klemperer after most of the water had been pumped out of the lake in October 1988 for a survey of the fish present. The photo also shows the concrete steps onto which the former starting boards could be man handled until 1957 so as to be at the waters edge. These steps are still there under the water.

Fig. 2.16 Dog tooth calcite crystals in the limestone wall of the so-called cave at Henleaze Lake. There are similar outcrops in Pen Park Hole, a huge cavern a mile north of the lake. The club's cave is situated opposite the club house on the other side of the drive. In former times it boasted a lean-to and was a genteel place to have your tea, away from the lake-side hubbub. (photo Mark Thompson)

gunner in action was generally reckoned to be in minutes. Long-standing club members (including the authors) will fondly remember Doug expertly coaching the springboard and the 10 metre platform divers. There was also a springboard above a sandpit which was used for diving practice, unlike the play sandpit installed for toddlers at the turn of the twenty-first century. The dry-land springboard has long gone but its concrete plinth and the remains of the sandpit could still be found under the brambles and nettles in 2005 to the north of the ladies' changing rooms. In 2006 a raised flower bed was created over the old plinth, appropriately using the toddlers' sandpit frame to confine the bed.

One can also still trace out the floor area in front of the so-called cave where the lean-to designed by Doug Satherley used to be. The cave is a hollow in the east cliff opposite the superintendents' hut and in its hey day it was an attractive, cool and shady place to sit and have your tea. The cave, incidentally, is one of the best places to see clusters of dog tooth calcite crystals protruding from the limestone cliff wall (Fig. 2.16).

Club Membership and Activities, Formation of Bristol Henleaze Swimming Club

During the early years after the war the membership of the lake averaged 800 but visitors numbered between 2,000 and 4,000, rather less than half being swimmers – the international competitions and galas for example attracted large crowds who would pay an entrance fee at the gate. There were no checks on guests' ability to swim, let alone requests to produce swimming certificates or to sign a disclaimer. The visiting teams of swimmers and divers were usually accommodated in the building known as The Royal School of Industry For The Blind just across Southmead Road from the lake. In 1946, however, when the English Inter-District Water Polo Tournament was held at Henleaze Lake some 40 officials and team players were accommodated and fed in Clifton College.

Much festive gear would be in evidence amongst the spectators at these galas but for the competitors regulation ASA costumes were *de rigeur*. In 1950 more relaxed regulations for costumes were introduced. Males now wore swimming costumes or trunks with drawers underneath. The legs reached no less than 3 inches below the crotch and were cut in a straight line around the circumference of the leg. Female costumes were 'of one piece, devoid of open work except at the back' and, as in the ruling for males, the legs reached no less than 3 inches below the crotch and were cut in a straight line. But female costumes were also cut 'not more than $4^1/2$ inches from the pit of the neck in front and not more then 2 inches from the crease of the arm in front', the object being 'to debar immodest costumes'. And it was felt necessary to rule that 'the texture of swimming costumes shall be non-transparent'; certainly, it was still a long way off the bikini.

During the 1950s the membership numbers, the great enthusiasm, and the successes in the competitive events very slowly but inexorably started to decline. Despite the extra income from dances (dances were held every month at St. Peter's Church Hall during 1952) and catering, escalating maintenance costs were having a serious effect on club finances. As always, some repairs and maintenance were carried out by a few willing members but this still left the expenses of replacing equipment and installing security measures. Water polo matches, however, were still very much part of club scene as shown by the impressive list of matches scheduled in 1958 (Fig. 2.17).

In the 1960s, swimming club membership averaged 470, with a low of 324 in 1966 (cp. Fig. 3.1 in Chapter 3). Fishing was disbanded in 1966 but re-started the following year under the auspices of Bob Steel, the celebrated club member (officer, and trustee) who swam in the lake every day of the year, sometimes breaking the ice to achieve this. Bob started daily year-round swimming in the River Yare while he lived in Norwich. One morning he cut himself up badly by inadvertently swimming through thin into thick ice. Moving to Bristol after the war he continued to swim daily in Henleaze Lake at 7 a.m. He disliked rain more than the winter cold and darkness, sometimes getting wet through on his walk to his home in Hill View. Bob, who lived to be 90, is also remembered as a geranium enthusiast. Every spring he planted a splendid array of many-shaded geraniums in the flower beds in front of

HENLEAZE SWIMMING CLUB

President: A. MACFARLANE, Esq.

Hon. Secretary: P. M. Leishman, 92 Monks Park Avenue, Bristol 7

Hon. Competition Secretary: E. A. Iles, 10 Shaldon Road, Bristol 7 (Tel. 65-2500)

WATER POLO

Date	Opponents	Team	Venue	Result
Mar. 20	Q.E.H.	Jun.	Away	
,, 21	B.G.S.	Jun.	Home	
,, 28	Bristol North	1st	Home	
Apr. 18	Barton Hill	2nd	Home	
,, 25	Central	1st	Home	
May 1	Cardiff	1st	Away	
,, 9	Q.E.H.	Jun.	Home	
,, 16	B.G.S. (B.L.)	Jun.	Away	
,, 16	Bath Dolphin	1st	Home	
,, 23	Central	Jun.	Home	
,, 28	B.A.C. (B.L.)	Jun.	Away	
,, 29	Q.E.H. (B.L.)	Jun.	Away	
,, 30	Cardiff	1st	Home	
,, 30	Cardiff	Jun.	Home	
June 5	Barton Hill (B.L.)	1st	Away	
,, 6	Bristol City	Jun.	Home	
,, 7	Stroud	2nd	Home★	
,, 10	Bath Dolphin (B.L.)	1st	Away	
,, 11	Central	Jun.	Home★	
,, 13	Gloucester (G.C.)	1st	Away	
,, 17	Gloucester	1st	Home★	
,, 18	B.A.C. (B.L.)	Jun.	Home★	
,, 18	Cardiff v. Bristol (Empire Pool)		Away	
,, 20	Bristol City	Jun.	Away	
,, 22	Central	1st	Home★	
,, 22	Central	Jun.	Home★	
,, 25	R.A.P.C. T.C. Devizes	1st	Home★	
,, 25	Q.E.H. (B.L.)	Jun.	Home★	
,, 27	B.G.S. (B.L.)	Jun.	Away	
,, 28	Cheltenham " A "	1st	Home★	
,, 28	Cheltenham (G.C.)	Jun.	Home★	
July 1	Frome (B.L.)	1st	Away	
,, 2	Barton Hill (B.L.)	1st	Home★	
,, 3	Cardiff	1st	Away	
,, 5	Cardiff	1st	Home★	
,, 8	Bristol North (B.L.)	1st	Home★	
,, 9	B.G.S. (B.L.)	Jun.	Home★	
,, 14	Weston-s.-Mare (B.L.)	1st	Away	
,, 16	Central (B.L.)	1st	Home★	
,, 18	Cheltenham " A "	1st	Away	
,, 19	Newport	1st	Home★	
,, 23	Weston-s.-Mare (B.L.)	1st	Home★	
,, 24	Bristol North (B.L.)	1st	Away	
,, 30	Bristol City (B.L.)	1st	Home★	
,, 31	Central	Jun.	Away	
Aug. 13	Frome (B.L.)	1st	Home★	
,, 20	Bath Dolphin (B.L.)	1st	Home★	

WATER POLO (continued).

Date	Opponents	Team	Venue	Result
Aug. 21	Barton Hill	1st	Away	
,, 26	Cirencester	1st	Home★	
,, 28	Barnstaple	1st	Away	
,, 29	Ilfracombe	1st	Away	
,, 30	Padstow	1st	Away	
Sept. 5	Bristol North	2nd	Home	
,, 12	Bristol City (B.L.)	1st	Away	
,, 18	Bristol North	2nd	Away	
,, 19	Central	1st	Home	
,, 25	Central (B.L.)	1st	Away	
,, 26	Barton Hill	1st	Home	

TEAM SWIMS

(Junior Team Swims at all (B.L.) matches)

Date	Opponents	Team	Venue	Result
May 19	Bath Dolphin	Women	Away	
,, 30	Cardiff	Men	Home	
,, 30	Cardiff	Jun.	Home	
June 6	Bristol City	Jun.	Home	
,, 13	Gloucester	Men	Away	
,, 13	Gloucester	Women	Away	
,, 17	Gloucester	Men	Home	
,, 17	Gloucester	Women	Home	
July 19	Newport	Men	Home	
Aug. 20	Bath Dolphin	Men	Home	
,, 26	Cirencester	Men	Home	
,, 26	Cirencester	Women	Home	

B.L. Bristol and District Water Polo League Match.

G.C. Gloucester County Championship.

★ Match to be played at Lake.

Fig. 2.17 The 1958 Henleaze Swimming Club fixtures list for water polo matches and team swims. To play over 50 polo matches during the season and, of course, to practise hard for them as well was nothing unusual in the 'olden' days. Ernie Iles was the club's Hon. Competition Secretary at this time. He and his wife Maisie ran the Competition Section for many years.

the superintendents' hut. Before Bob, Dr Green was also known for daily year-round swimming in the lake, often running there in shorts during the winter before taking the plunge.

A new replacement raft was launched at 50 yards distance from the starting board in July 1961 and a retaining embankment running from the diving tower to the starting board was built to secure and improve the east bank. Events such as a barbecue and a motor car treasure hunt were organised in order to boost the funds but by 1966 the club was in grave danger of closing down after running into a serious financial situation. Dances were discontinued in 1959, although the club did arrange a barn dance in 1997 and again in 1998. No diving championships were held at the lake after 1963 and water polo at the lake ceased in 1968 after struggling for several years to put on a team.

Neil Murison, who was the polo captain for several years, recalls that to field his polo team of seven players he really needed eleven active players so that sufficient reserves were always on hand. The game can get quite violent (Neil Murison suffered two burst ear drums) so that players would normally be toughened up in the junior teams before moving up to join the seniors. However, in the late 1950s a shortage of junior Henleaze players meant that as senior polo players moved away they were no longer being replaced; finally a senior polo team could no longer be mustered. Competitive swimming in the lake suffered a similar fate but for different reasons. As championship records continued to fall and times and distances became more precise the difficulties of setting specific and reproducible competition facilities in open water became apparent.

Another factor affecting high achievement is the water temperature which can obviously hinder performance if it is too low. One old polo team member recalls how at one polo match the water was so cold that if one member of a team got in and put the ball into the net they could have the match! Water needs to be at a reasonable temperature if competitors are to give of their best and Henleaze Lake, in common with other open waters in this country, is rarely a match for heated indoor pools. Furthermore the lengthy periods of training now demanded of competitors year round pretty well cuts out training in open water. At any rate competition swimming, like competition diving, waned at the lake. One factor affecting this was the inability of would-be competitors to join in on the day. No traditional gala days were held at Henleaze Lake after 1983.

The difficulties that beset competitive swimming at the lake were exacerbated by some other problems which combined to encourage the club's Indoor Section to go its own way. Already in 1969 a separate sub-committee had been formed to oversee teaching, training, and competitive events of the Competitive Section as it came to be known. Training took place in the lake during the summer months and at Bristol North Baths all the year round. After 1983, which is the year of the last gala held at Henleaze Lake, the section's training activities moved entirely to Bristol North Baths. Nevertheless competition venues and results were always read out at meetings of the swimming club's executive committee. Training had been taking place at Bristol North Baths since the club's inception in 1919 and the first of the club's championship trophies was given to the club in 1920. Training continued at Bristol North Baths until the baths closed on 23 October 2006, and moved to Horfield Leisure Centre Pool and Clifton High School Pool.

From 1983 onwards the Competitive Section grew in strength with increasing numbers of swimmers, supporters, and coaches, whilst competitive swimming at the lake was non-existent. There is little interest in the Amateur Swimming Association and competitive swimming amongst Henleaze Swimming Club members because a high proportion of them are purely recreational swimmers who like to enjoy the lake on a nice sunny day.

At a Special General Meeting on 15 December 1992 the Competitive Section decided formally to become a separate club – Bristol Henleaze Swimming Club – and fission of Henleaze Swimming Club occurred on 1 January 1993. Due to the two clubs having similar names, swimming officials sometimes confuse the two and the HSC Hon. Secretary sometimes receives BHSC mail in error. Indeed, some people still think BHSC and HSC are one and the same club.

On the other hand, a close relationship between BHSC and HSC is still necessary and is actively fostered. HSC may have stopped making an annual payment to BHSC funds, as it did for many years, but HSC concessions are extended to BHSC members and they enjoy an annual barbecue at the lake. Since 1999 BHSC members swim alongside HSC members in the Gloucester County ASA Open Water Championship events which are now held at the lake every year. Many officials for these events are provided by both HSC and BHSC.

HSC made a donation towards the considerable expenses of BHSC's successful relay swim from England to France and back in under 24 hours, on 27/28 July 2004. This powerful event was managed by Judith Bush, the BHSC chief coach who swam in a school Channel relay team in 1970 and nearly managed to swim the Channel by herself the following year when she was 15 years old. The two big problems in Channel swimming, she says, are seasickness and lack of sleep. The BHSC Channel relay swim substantially aided two local causes – The Bristol Union of Disability Sports and Frenchay Hospital's Specialist Burns Unit. The relay swimmers who performed this feat trained in Henleaze Lake. BHSC swimmers also trained in the lake for a triathlon event in 2005 and the Bristol and District Triatheletes (BadTri) have since then started training in their own right in Henleaze Lake.

We may note here that the lake is one of the few places where the Health and Safety Executive has allowed springboard and diving platform facilities to remain and where diving lessons can be obtained.

Some very wet and cold starts to the seasons in the late 1960s and early 1970s added to Henleaze Swimming Club's difficulties. In 1966 the lake was in danger of never opening due to the excess water which fully covered the car park but thanks due to the ingenuity of Bob Steel, 3 million gallons of water were pumped out. This was repeated the following year when steps had to be taken to provide a more permanent pumping system which we describe in Chapter 3. The new system became operational in 1969.

1968 proved to be one of the coldest summers on record but summer weather returned in 1969 and 1970. Membership improved slightly which funded some repairs and a second-hand caravan was purchased for the selling of refreshments which was run voluntarily by a band of willing lady helpers. The caravan was parked by the ladies changing room and the Hon. Club Secretary John White towed it home at closing time every evening to frustrate the vandals. A block booking for canoeing from the Bristol Education Authority also added a little to the funds.

During the seasons before and after the war the lake opened at 6 a.m. to enable keen swimmers to get in some training before going to work. Fred Allard and Bob Steel (who both lived to a great age) would be seen amongst others arriving daily for an early swim. Over the next few years, however, opening was delayed until 7.30 a.m., then 8 a.m. and finally in 1957 to 10 a.m. to reduce the long hours worked by the superintendents. Since 1976 the lake has been opened at 11 in the morning. As Dot Ridley née Brown has written of earlier years 'Young people today with their leisure centres and heated pools don't know what they are missing'. There was a trial opening of the lake on Fridays at 7.30 a.m. during July, August and September in 2004; this was deemed to be sufficiently successful for it to be continued in subsequent seasons and extended to include Fridays in June.

Problems of Intrusion onto Lake Property

Vandalism was always a problem and trespassers breaking into the north end of the lake property were difficult to control because there was no land access further than half way up the west side of the lake. When the weather was hot, it was not unusual to see numerous intruders on the sloping cliff face beyond the bay at the northern end of the lake where they would sunbathe and swim in the adjacent water, especially outside club opening hours. The intruders, who coexisted with club members but separated from them, normally kept to the northern reaches of the lake, although on one or two occasions did swim down and appear in the 'members' end'. On one occasion one of the authors swam up to the intruders and struck up a conversation. On being asked why they did not apply to join Henleaze Swimming Club the reply was to look at it this way: members pay to swim in the lake and intruders swim for free so who is better off?

The club archives reveal that three ex-government pontoons, each 20 ft long and 6 ft wide, were delivered to Henleaze Lake in 1949. There is, however, no record of their ever having been floated on the lake or what became of them. In any case, there was already a substantial raft anchored 50 yards up the lake from the starting board. With steps at each end, this raft had been a familiar and well-used feature at the lake since the 1930s. It is shown clearly in Fig. 1.24 in Chapter 1 and it served until 1957 when it was reconstructed; as we have stated, it was finally replaced with a new raft in 1961. Older members remember how the raft was constantly removed to the northern end by intruders and brought back by members of the club the next day. The intruders finally managed to break up the raft and ruin it in 1984; it has never been replaced. The loss of the raft in 1984 was cited as a reason for there being no club gala in 1984 because until then the corked rope lanes were strung between the starting board and the raft. The raft was, however, replaced for just one day in 2005 for the filming of *Nectar* (Colour Fig. 4.16) when a splendid raft which could easily have been made permanent graced the waters.

A steel perimeter fence, barbed wire fencing and a high unclimbable fence of metal palings were constructed in an attempt to keep out intruders; all were

CITY AND COUNTY OF BRISTOL

CITY ENGINEER & SURVEYOR'S OFFICE,
ARNO'S COURT,
470 BATH ROAD,
BRISTOL, 4.

J. B. BENNETT, M.I.C.E., M.I.Mun.E.,
CITY ENGINEER, SURVEYOR,
AND PLANNING OFFICER.

12th September, 19 58

Our Ref. WJ/EN/294/CE

Your Ref.

The Hon. Secretary,
Henleaze Swimming Club,
Lake Road,
Westbury-on-Trym,
Bristol.

Dear Sir,

Henleaze Lake

At a recent meeting the Parks Visiting Sub-Committee of the Planning and Public Works Committee considered the danger of serious accidents which exist at the Henleaze Lake at points to which access could be obtained from Badocks Wood. They noted that strong barbed wire fencing had been broken down and destroyed in several places and that a high unclimbable fence of metal palings which had been erected on a short length of the quarry boundary on a trial basis, had been deliberately breached by the removal of a number of palings.

They resolved that I should be requested to negotiate with your Club with a view to arrangements being made whereby the northern part of the Henleaze Lake may be filled by the Corporation by the tipping of inoffensive material within the area of the quarry, in order to eliminate the existing danger.

I shall be glad, therefore, if a meeting could be arranged at an early date between representatives of your Club and the Deputy City Engineer (Mr. W. Johnson) to discuss this matter. A mutually convenient time could be arranged by telephone.

Yours faithfully,

J. B. Bennett

City Engineer and Planning Officer

Fig. 2.18 This letter from the Bristol City Engineer and Planning Officer proposing to fill in the top end of the lake was sent to the club's Hon. Secretary in 1958. Club Trustees Fred Allard and Tony Elliott met with the authorities and were able to avert this unwelcome prospect. In fact, they managed to persuade the Corporation to erect a very substantial perimeter fence around the northern end of the lake property in 1960.

deliberately breached. The Mines & Quarries Act 1954 which came into force at the beginning of 1957 required the lake to provide an efficient and properly maintained barrier so designed and constructed as to prevent any persons from accidentally falling into the quarry. Tony Elliott, an active member and Honorary Club Solicitor for many years, accordingly wrote to Bristol Corporation pointing out that 'whatever action is taken to provide a fence, it has proved to be of no avail since the fencing is invariably broken down by hooligans who, I am informed, come from the corporation's tenanted houses'. He therefore 'respectfully suggested that the corporation should contribute to a large extent in erecting such a barrier as would give complete protection and will not require renewal and repair every few weeks', this being an expense which the club could no longer countenance.

In July 1957 Tony Elliott appeared at Bristol Juvenile Court to prosecute three boys for attempting to take fish from the lake. The case was proved and each boy ordered to pay a fine of five shillings. Costs were not granted and the boys made much of the fact that there was a gap in the fence. Breaches of the club's perimeter fences were also responsible for a number of tragic drownings which occurred among intruders.

In 1958 a teenage intruder died when he dived off the long wide sloping rock face at the far end of the lake and hit rocks. The upshot of this tragedy was that the City Engineer and Planning Officer proposed that the north end of Henleaze Lake should be filled in by the tipping of inoffensive material to prevent further accidents (Fig 2.18). Fred Allard and Tony Elliott were able to prevent this and persuaded the City Council in 1960 to erect a sturdy 8 feet tall fence around the northern end of the lake property where it abuts Badock Woods. This steel fence, which still stands today, cost £4,400 and the *Bristol Evening World* reported at the time that it would 'keep even Tarzan out'.

Amongst some 14 drowning tragedies at Henleaze Lake since the quarry flooded, no drowning of a club member has ever occurred. This is doubtlessly due to the club's first Rule which states that 'The Club shall be for swimmers only' and its enforcement via Rule 11 which lays down that 'an essential qualification for membership shall be the passing of the swimming test of 50 yards at Henleaze Lake'. The only two tragedies that have occurred amongst members since the club's inception in 1919 involved a diving accident and heart failure respectively. Intruders to the lake property, invariably after the lake was closed, have been the subject of all other tragic events. Many involved children and one was a double drowning. Over the years some animals have also drowned in the lake.

During the 1960s, 1970s and 1980s the club experienced much trouble from vandals. Intruders came through the gardens of Lakewood Road residents and the club's Executive Committee received many letters of complaints regarding not only the intruders but also the general behaviour of young club members. It could be guaranteed that any warm sunny day would be spoilt by the yobbish elements who invaded the lake, often with dogs. The lake anglers felt threatened and withdrew. The police made frequent visits during the summer of 1971 on foot, in Panda cars, and even in plain clothes. These visits proved to be very effective and a great help. A second lake superintendent was employed for the first time so that one could be at the entrance gate and one by the lake.

Vandalism took place every winter. During the winter of 1978/79 vandals managed to penetrate the superintendents' hut; the inflatable rubber boat was slashed, the telephone was broken, the tea urn filled with paint, and the clock together with sundry items were destroyed. A crime prevention officer was consulted and the hut was strengthened by building a concrete block wall inside the metal sheet cladding. The roof was treated with anti-climb paint.

The police were again consulted during the 1981 season but this time the advice was 'to play it cool' in view of the riots which had taken place in other parts of the country! A uniformed security guard was employed which improved the situation for a while. In 1982 a gate was constructed on the path at the end of the swimming area and a security guard was employed again, improving the situation for a while. This gate became known as the Meehan Gate because it was the idea of Clare Meehan, one of the club trustees. Two student guards were employed during the summers of 1983 and 1984. However, some very ugly occasions occurred in 1984 when a superintendent was threatened with a knife and a student guard was chased by thugs to Southmead police station where he sought refuge. Court injunctions were taken out against three of the worst offenders. This was a costly procedure for the club which was impecunious at the time but the individuals did not visit the lake again and the trespass subsided.

The problems of intrusion and vandalism have been brought to a very low level in more recent times and the smooth running of the club has hardly been disturbed since the 1990s. Undoubtedly the biggest single factor to bring this about has been the construction by the anglers in 1988 of a path and boardwalks which give access from 'The Point' half way along the lake to within casting distance of the far northern end. At the same time the boundary fences of the property were substantially improved with anti-intrusion measures. These developments, together with a day and night presence of anglers and bailiffs at the lake meant that the lake was now rarely deserted over its entire length for the whole of the year.

There have, on occasions, been justified complaints about the behaviour of bona fide swimming members (whose membership was proposed and seconded) and anglers. Sometimes superintendents' accounts or letters reach the committee describing such sins as abandoned guests, teenage ruffians running about noisily, swimming in sawn-off jeans, spitting, loud bad language, and shouted verbal abuse. Less frequently a more serious situation erupts; in 1979 a committee member and three guests 'were seen to be running and dancing about on the grass beyond the high diving stage in the nude'. Sharp intake of breath. Requests to desist and put some clothes on only evoked torrents of pretty foul language directed at the complainants.

This appears to have been a difficult period for club discipline because in 1981 38 members signed a request for a General Meeting 'to discuss the trespassers and general behaviour at the lake'. Again, the minutes of the August 1993 committee meeting and several letters describe how about a dozen members insisted on continuing an unauthorised barbecue with the result that a fracas broke out with much attendant distress. Two family memberships were withdrawn in the aftermath and the superintendent on duty at the time was sacked. Even less desirable was a serious fracas which broke out amongst anglers in 2005; it resulted in blood on the boardwalks and the ejection of angling members from the Fishing Section. But enough of unsavoury truths about what is really a very genteel club 99% of the time.

Some Recollections from The Halcyon Post-War Years

Peter Allard (Fred Allard's son) has written of the early post-war years.

I have given some thought to activities at the lake when I was a member years ago. Bunty Cartridge is one of the names that comes to mind. She was a very good swimmer and used to live close to the lake, but I believe she moved just before she retired from British Aerospace. The Murison brothers were very keen members. One was a diver and I believe he was a doctor in Bath. The other brother, Neil, was a brilliant back stroke swimmer and today he is a well known artist in Bristol.

The Jennings and the McGowan families put a lot of time and effort into the club. Ernie Jennings was a director of Cadena Cake Shops and his wife worked very hard organising the tea hut. She had a good team which included my mother and they always made a profit for the club. However, a certain Pat Jacklin came along and thought she could do it better so the old team disappeared and it was never the same. The dances at St Peter's Hall were always very popular and again my parents worked hard at these functions as well. My mother's egg sandwiches were always in demand.

Swimming galas were the highlights of the year and were very popular with the public. The teams from Bristol Central used to be the ones to beat. Their swimmers were brilliant and one in particular was Ray Legg – no one stood a chance against him. Just after the war there was a gala with an international flavour, England vs. Sweden. The polo match (cp Figs. 1.9, 2.2, 2.3 and 2.17) was a walkover for Sweden; they won 9–1. The England goal was a result of a penalty and no one argued about it. The Swedish team was really smart and all their members were dressed in blue and yellow.

★ ★ ★

57 years after the Swedish team visited Henleaze Lake a then young lady writes 'I remember one year when the Swedish team came to practise for the Olympics – all gorgeous brown men! We had a lovely time!!' The divers and water polo teams were accommodated and well looked after at the Royal School for the Blind (see Fig. 1.6 in Chapter 1) which was situated opposite Old Quarry Park on the other side of Henleaze Road, some 200 metres from the lake. We have earlier referred to the swimming pool which existed in the school's grounds and was filled in after the school was closed and sold in 1969. The school, which had been open since 1911 was demolished with explosives in 1971 and the clock tower now only chimes out the hours in the mind's ear of those with a long memory.

CHAPTER 3
THE LEAN YEARS, FISHING AND WATER QUALITY

post tenebras lux

Low Membership Numbers and a Worrying Financial Period

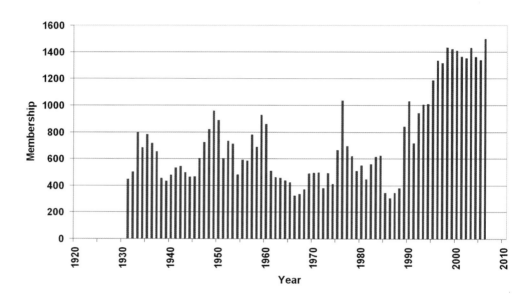

Fig. 3.1 Henleaze Swimming Club membership numbers up to 2006, taken from the club's Annual Reports.

Fig. 3.1 shows how the number of members in the swimming club fell away during the 1960s and again in the 1980s. The gravity of the club's predicament in 1964, when there were 437 members, is recorded in a letter written to the Hon. Secretary by the club's Hon. Solicitor and Trustee: 'in this period in the club's history it is a struggle to keep going'. Two years later there were only 324 club members but then a gradual recovery began. For the 24 years 1961 to 1984 membership averaged 516 but in the following four years, 1985 to 1988, the average fell to 345, falling to an all-time low of 307 members in 1986.

These low membership numbers coupled with a financial deficit for each the years 1981 to 1987 prompted the executive committee to appeal for donations and to hold an Open Day at the lake in 1986 (Figs. 3.2 left and right) and 1987. Leaflets

Fig. 3.2 *Left:* The leaflet announcing an Open Day at Henleaze Lake in 1986 was distributed to numerous local houses. The programme included demonstrations of swimming, diving, and life saving. A second Open Day was held in 1987 in a desperate attempt to boost membership numbers. *Right:* This photograph was taken at the 1986 Open Day at Henleaze Lake and shows some of the stalls. Visitors were able to walk along the edge of the Lake into the area normally reserved for anglers only. There was a good attendance despite blustery weather. (photo Derek Klemperer)

advertising these Open Days were hand delivered to a large number of local homes; the public were invited to see what we do and how we do it. Curiously advertising for the third and final Open Day in 1988 was suppressed; there was not even a notice on the entrance gate, suggesting poor committee support for the venture.

During his 18 years as the club's Hon. Secretary and until his death in 1987, John White organised house-to-house collections of jumble, explaining to householders by word of mouth and handbills (Fig. 3.3) that the jumble sales would help children learn to swim; in those days there was no national curriculum that included swimming for schools. The club's Indoor Section or Competition Section, as it came to be called, was still very much a part of Henleaze Swimming Club at that time. Indeed John White was strongly associated with the Competition Section and he would dutifully bring all the club's championship cups and trophies to the AGM every year for redistribution. The plinths were always engraved with the reigning champions' names. The jumble sales were held at St. Andrews Church Hall on Pigsty Hill, 16a Gloucester Road. At the same time John consistently opposed raising the club's membership subscription. Even the Annual Reports and Opening Notices were distributed amongst the Executive Committee members for delivery by hand in order to save money.

The wonderful summer of 1976 briefly improved the club's fortunes with a membership of 1035 – a record up to that time despite the low level of the lake water. Advantage was taken of the low water level to extend the concrete retaining wall of the swimming area beyond the diving tower. This major work enabled the rocky area back from the lake edge shown in Fig. 3.4 to be built up and lawned over. This improved both the safety and the appearance of the water's edge. At the same time a concrete retaining wall was constructed on the opposite side of the lake.

HENLEAZE SWIMMING CLUB

Affiliated to : Western Counties A.S.A.
Gloucester County A.S.A.
Royal Life Saving Society

JUMBLE SALE

Do you know that Henleaze Swimming Club teaches over 100 non-swimmers to swim each year and provides instructors and Coaches to enable these Swimmers to reach County and even International standards.

This means hiring Swimming Baths, which we do on three evenings a week throughout the year. This is a very expensive item, although all instruction is given on a voluntary basis.

We are therefore going to run a Jumble Sale to raise funds and will be pleased to collect any articles you can spare, Clothes, Woollens, Books, Ornaments, etc.

Collectors will be calling on Thursday evening next.

PLEASE HELP with this worthwhile work.

THANK YOU.

J. H. White,
Hon. Secretary,
Lea House,
Station Lane,
Muller Road,
Bristol. BS7 9NB

Tel - 653911

Fig.3.3 One of the handbills that was circulated to householders during the 1970s announcing that jumble would be collected by the club. Sales of this jumble raised money to pay for the hire of indoor baths at which club volunteers taught youngsters to swim.

Fig. 3.4 The rocky lake edge beyond the diving tower prior to the construction of concrete embankments and a lawn in 1976. (photo Bob Teesdale)

Nevertheless the long hot summer of 1976 was blighted when a boy who had been swimming in the lake contracted Weil's disease and the lake was closed for a fortnight (described later in this chapter). Although the source of infection could not be traced to lake water despite extensive water analysis, the ensuing publicity undoubtedly contributed to a down turn in the club's fortunes after 1976. Even years later one still hears people commenting 'Oh, that was the lake that had Weil's disease', when perhaps they know nothing else about the club.

Further possible causes for a decline in the club's membership numbers in the 1960s and 1980s may be adduced by the historian in addition to those that we have mentioned. The executive committee members and the club's trustees were aging during these lean years; they may have experienced a recession in their attention to club affairs and their voluntary efforts as evidenced, for instance, by cessation of beating the bounds after 1968. In 1984 the Hon. Solicitor and Trustee Tony Elliott wrote to two of his Trustee colleagues who had moved out of Bristol asking them formally to resign being trustees so that new trustees could be approached. Then there is evidence that the system of proposing and seconding applications for swimming club membership (this has never existed for fishing membership applications) was not always applied impartially leading, one senses, to detrimental ramifications. We mention two typical examples. As a boy, Ken Mitchell (who died in 2006) was refused admission to membership of the Club for several years because he was a better swimmer than the Club Chairman's son and would be able to beat him in competition swimming. And Dave O'Reilly, currently one of our fishing bailiffs, was only admitted to the club as a boy by giving his grandmother's address to the Executive Committee. Dave's real address was in Southmead and anyone with a Southmead address stood no chance of getting into the club at that time. Finally, starting in the 1950s, membership falls could be due to the public's increasing mobility with cars; this would make attractions outside Bristol more accessible. Ironically, vehicle congestion on the roads may have brought about the opposite effect towards the end of the millennium.

In any event, the Executive Committee and the Trustees failed to meet the escalating maintenance costs and there were operating deficits in 1975, 1976 and 1977 and again, as we have stated, for the years 1981 to 1987. Meanwhile the club's Fishing Section viewed the situation in the swimming club with misgivings. The Fishing Section was very much a going concern in the 1980s with a lot of effort being put in by the anglers. Predictably, the anglers sought a formal assurance from the swimming club that fishing at Henleaze Lake would be allowed to continue whatever happened to the swimming club. In a letter dated 12 January 1988 the swimming club's Hon. Solicitor Tony Elliott was unable to give this assurance because 'It is quite conceivable that for financial reasons the swimming club might have to cease activities at the lake'. The authors recall having a serious talk with Tony Elliott about how the club property might be sold and who the beneficiaries would be. This must be the only area the club's founding fathers did not clarify in the otherwise most carefully drafted deed of purchase in 1933.

The seriousness of the situation prompted the authors to send an open letter to the club's Trustees and the Chairman of the Committee in November 1987 (Fig. 3.5). This letter, which was thankfully acted upon, pointed out the club's serious financial position and recommended corrective measures. But it was not until Carol Holloway became Acting Hon. Secretary in 1988 (and one of the club's long serving Hon. Secretaries the following year) that a turnaround took effect. The membership figures for 1989 to 2004 average 1197, in marked contrast to the earlier years. Indeed for the nine years up to 2004, membership always exceeded 1300 and capping of the membership number was introduced together with a waiting list of applicants.

Since the summer of 1995 when the water temperature reached 77 °F (25 °C) membership numbers have consistently been high, reaching an all-time record of 1497 members in 2006, more by happenstance than design because enrolling members is a pipeline process. Nevertheless membership cannot comfortably exceed a target figure of 1350 because the lawns impose a physical limit. On a hot weekend day in July and August one has to pick one's way carefully through sunbathing members and their guests laid out on the lawns. When reviewing membership numbers the Matthew effect becomes apparent (To him that hath shall be given). After a good year, membership renewals are issued in the following year to all those who were members in the previous year so that numbers tend to increase automatically.

The popularity of Henleaze Lake is testimony to the absence nowadays of any other place like it in and around Bristol. Keynes Country Park near Cirencester is probably the nearest attractive open water swimming that is available to the public.

HENLEAZE SWIMMING CLUB

Affiliated to

Western Counties A.S.A.   Gloucester County A.S.A.   Royal Life Saving Society

President:
D. KLEMPERER

Hon. Secretary	_Hon. Competition Secretary:_	_Hon. Treasurer:_	_Fishing Secretary:_
J.H. WHITE	Mrs. M. HARRIS	Mrs. M.C. MEEHAN	Mr. & Mrs. KLEMPERER
Lea House,	18 Mayfield Park,	157 Knole Lane,	25 Rockside Drive,
Station Lane,	Fishponds,	Bristol BS10 6JP	Henleaze,
Muller Road,	Bristol BS16 3NN.	Tel. 503685	Bristol BS9 4NU
Bristol BS7 9NB.	Tel. 654070		Tel. 623748
Tel. 516407			

1st November 1987.

ANNUAL STATEMENT OF ACCOUNTS 1987.

We refer to the request for views concerning the financing of the Club in the 1987 Annual Report. We are sure that all members of the Henleaze Swimming Club as well as the Committee are concerned and worried that this is the 6th year with an operating deficit. This year the deficit was again over £1,000 and the balance in the Building Society and Bank now adds up to not much more than twice this year's loss. This is a serious situation that merits serious action.

The wage bill + P.A.Y.E. for the five summer months amounts to £4,500. We submit that unless this expense is considerably reduced we are putting the very existence of Henleaze Swimming Club in jeopardy.

The Swimming Club survives very well with one superintendent throughout September and we see no reason why this arrangement cannot be extended into other summer months. We should like to propose the following throughout the 1988 season:

(1)   2 Superintendents every Saturday and Sunday. This would allow time for grass cutting and routine work to be done as there are many weekends when it is quiet at the Lake.

(2)   1 Superintendent for each week day.

In the past men like Mr. Lampert and Mr. Britten (with his dog) successfully supervised the Lake on their own with a larger membership than we have now. We do not recommend a major rise in subscriptions to meet the deficit.

Yours sincerely

Derek F. Klemperer   Joyce F. Klemperer

Open letter to the Trustees of Henleaze Swimming Club and Chairman for the Executive Committees 1987 and 1988.

Fig. 3.5 This open letter was sent to the club's Trustees and the Chairman of the Committee in November 1987. It points out the very serious financial situation that the swimming club was in and is really a plea for survival. Thankfully, the measures proposed were acted upon.

Development of Fishing at the Lake

Income from fishing at Henleaze Lake makes a major contribution to club income. Fig. 3.6 shows how the ratio of fishing income to swimming income has varied since the war. In constructing this bar chart we have excluded several grants that were attracted for site improvements. From 1989 to 2005 the income from fishing was maintained at a steady proportion of close to 20% of swimming income but in 2006 the proportion fell to 15% as a result of large swimming guest numbers attracted by the excellent and sustained summer weather. In the years before 1989, fishing contributed a higher proportion. In the 1970s and 80s the proportion often exceeded 50%, reaching a record 86% in 1981. The period of high percentages coincides with the 18 years during which John White was Hon. Secretary of the swimming club. It was during his time that the club experienced lean years of poor swimming income, culminating in near collapse.

After World War One Major Badock was the lessee of Southmead Lake, as it was then known. He stocked the water with trout so that he and his friends could enjoy fishing there, continuing after Henleaze Swimming Club was formed in 1919. In 1924 Major Badock purchased the lake property and, as we have described in Chapter 1, the club was able to purchase the property from him in 1933. The deed

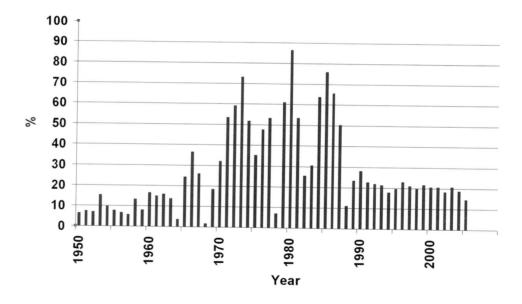

Fig. 3.6 Fishing income as a percentage of swimming income over the years since the war up to 2006. An average of 20% has been maintained over the years of good swimming income since 1990. Prior to that and for some 20 years the higher percentages shown are a reflection of the swimming club's low membership numbers and poor income. A formal Fishing Section of Henleaze Swimming Club with a Secretary and Treasurer was not set up until 1967 although pay-at-the-gate day fishing had been offered for a long time prior to this.

of purchase specifies that during his lifetime Major Badock reserved for himself and his friends 'the sole and exclusive right of fishing and boating on any part of the lake'. He died in 1945 and fishing under the auspices of the swimming club started in a small informal way.

Ten members who no longer swam were granted permission to fish the lake and this permission was passed on to others as those of the original ten anglers ceased to fish. The number of anglers was kept at ten. At that time, and indeed until 1987, there was no land access to the lake edge north of the rocky point situated half way along the west (Lakewood Road) side. Fish stocks were also very poor, being limited largely to roach, although there were some trout and a few carp in the lake. The carp must have been introduced by Major Badock before the war. If the fish looked healthy, then the water was deemed to be acceptable for swimmers – an early *ad hoc* manner of observing water quality amongst members.

The earliest record of stocking dates from 1950 when the swimming club purchased Loch Leven trout and placed them in the lake. Trout were then added each spring in subsequent years. In 1952 the record shows that stocking was with 'trout and fresh water shrimps'. Fishing fees first appear in the accounts for 1951. Fishing by people who paid at the gate for a day's fishing was the source of this income and day fishing continued to be offered at Henleaze Lake right up to 1987. In that year the bailiffs stopped day fishing to ensure that high quality private fishing would be provided only for subscribing members and their guests in a secure and peaceful environment.

By 1957 anglers were pointing out that the lake afforded limited facilities when compared with other waters that they fished, and that fishing was only allowed when the lake was closed for swimming. A lot of fishing occurred at all times by intruders in the isolated northern regions of the lake. Little was done to improve the situation although swimming member Arthur Haley tried to gather together some 12 fly fishermen who fished at the lake and form a club. In later years Arthur has became a familiar sight sitting on the swimming club lawns wearing his inimitable straw hat, blazer, tie, and flannels, even on a hot day. Fly fishing, however, was frustrated by the very large number of roach in the lake which led to the lake being netted three times in 1963. Several thousand roach were taken out and placed into local rivers. Nevertheless fishing continued to be poor and in 1965 the suggestion was made that fishing activities at the lake should be changed from purely trout fishing to mixed fishing by the introduction of coarse fish.

The first formal fishing report features in the swimming club's Annual Report for 1966. The report stated that Laurie McGowan, the swimming club Hon. Secretary who looked after fishing matters, had died and the remaining anglers had decided 'to disband the fishing activities'. In the following year the swimming club's Hon. Treasurer Bob Steel (of daily year round swimming fame) proposed that a Coarse Fishing Section of Henleaze Swimming Club be set up with a subscribing membership maximum of 60 and a set of Fishing Rules (Fig. 3.7).

Since the swimming club's inception and up to 1967 fishing at the lake was the province of a very small number of (official) anglers. Now, however, numbers were to increase. The new Fishing Section was up and running in 1968 with Bob Steel at

HENLEAZE SWIMMING CLUB

Dear *Mr Davis*

The Committee of the Henleaze Swimming Club have given some thought to the formation of a Coarse Fishing Section at Henleaze Lake and have come to the conclusion that before doing so, the lake should be better stocked with a wider variety of fish.

In addition to the Trout and Roach already in the Lake, it has been decided to add 200 four to six inch Carp and 200 three to five inch Tench, which should thrive and provide good sport. Unfortunately, delivery of these additional fish of the size we require cannot be obtained before next winter. In consequence, it has been decided to continue this summer with fishing on a daily basis, during the hours the Lake is open for swimming, at five shillings per day as from Saturday the 17th June, until the Lake closes for swimming on Sunday the 1st October. Thereafter it will be open for fishing only on Sundays from 10-00a.m. until 5-00p.m., until December 10th, or until such time as flood conditions make fishing undesirable, whichever is the earlier.

I enclose a copy of the draft Rules for the Fishing Section which it is proposed to adopt to give you an idea of the lines on which the Committee is thinking. I should be glad to have any comments you care to make, as it is the Committee's aim to provide good fishing under reasonable conditions. I should also like to know whether you wish to join the Section in 1968, under the proposed conditions, so that we can see the extent to which it is likely to be supported.

In the meantime, the Committee thank you for your support last year and look forward to seeing you and your angling friends on the daily basis during the coming season.

Yours faithfully,

Fig. 3.7 The letter that was sent out to known day anglers of Henleaze Lake in June 1967 seeking their support for a proposed Coarse Fishing Section of Henleaze Swimming Club with the swimming club's Hon. Treasurer Bob Steel at the helm. The response was good and the first subscribing fishing members paid their dues in 1968. At the same time day fishing at the lake continued to be a feature.

the helm until his retirement in 1982. In that year the authors became the first Hon. Fishing Secretaries and Treasurers, a joint post they held single-handedly for 23 years before gratefully taking on extra help with the work. As José Marti, the father of Cuban independence has remarked, long service obliges you to continue serving; it is a situation Alan Giles, Chairman of the Executive Committee also understands only too well.

Disaster struck in 1969 when a highly contagious disease killed most of the fish in the lake. The Bristol and Avon River Authority examined three dead roach and found that they were infected with *Aeromanas formicans* and *Cytophaga columnaris*. The Authority's advice was to ban fishing and let the disease take its course. Dead fish were scooped off the surface of the water, seemingly day after day, and Graham Twiggs the swimming club's Hon. Secretary at that time carted them away for disposal in wheelbarrow loads. This sobering experience demonstrated to everyone how lethal disease can occur if fish stocks are not kept in isolation and only added to after a licence to move has been obtained. This ensures that fish additions are healthy. After a hiatus stocking was restarted, notably with trout that were placed in the water every spring until 1990.

In 1987/88 an energetic and dedicated subscribing fishing membership took on the Herculean task of extending the access for anglers to the northern half of Henleaze Lake. Until 1987 there was only access to the waters edge half way along the lake, the northern half being bounded by cliffs that plunged straight into deep water. In the first phase of this work 40 tons of earth and rock were built up to make a path around the bay, then a cantilevered boardwalk was affixed to the projecting cliff face at the end of the bay path and finally a scaffold boardwalk was constructed to within casting distance of the end of the lake. The whole work was completed within a year and considerably helped by generous grants from the Sports Council and Bristol City Council.

Angling member Keith Pickett provided the cantilevered walkway and Steve and Chris Cottrell installed the scaffold for the final boardwalk. Many others helped whilst at the same time the swimming club's run-down club house was refurbished for use; a new roof was given by Les Claridge, a fishing section sponsor and benefactor for several years. The perimeter fences of the lake property were also considerably strengthened by fishing members. The anglers removed some 15 tons of rubbish from the lake floor at the time of the Wessex Water Authority's pump down in October 1988 (described below) following up with the introduction of oxygen-giving Canadian pond weed to the restored water.

During this period of vigour and enthusiasm matches were staged regularly and the anglers held a number of social functions. At a discotheque in Westbury village hall in 1986 the shield, trophies and a cup donated by Les Claridge were awarded. In 1988 an anglers' barbecue was held at the Beehive Public House and a skittles match was arranged.

As a consequence of the increased access to the waters edge, the number of senior anglers who could be comfortably accommodated was increased from 100 (Bob Steel's original 60 had already risen steadily to 100) to 160 and finally 180. It is interesting to note that out of the senior membership the number of women members has never exceeded eight. The junior angling membership has never been large; it fluctuates between 20 and 40 and juniors are always taken at once in accordance with a policy of encouraging them. The bailiffs are particularly good with juniors, helping them by loaning equipment and giving instruction.

In 1991 the bailiffs and anglers constructed several swims (places to fish from in fishing parlance) along the west bank (Lakewood Road side) of the lake to the south of 'The Point'. These swims, for which a mechanical digger was hired, were constructed of earth and rocks, held in place by metal netting and old lorry tyres. They largely deteriorated over the course of the next 15 years and are due to be gradually replaced by stone maintenance-free structures keyed into the bank. To each swim is added a flight of steps down to the water so that the fish can be gently replaced into the lake after being caught and perhaps weighed, photographed, and entered in the Catch Book. As Colour Fig. 3.1 shows, properly constructed swims are not visible from the water and in no way detract from the beauty of the 'natural-looking' lake banks.

At the time of the major works of access to the water the fishing club had no less than eight bailiffs, all doing good work. Nevertheless inevitable power struggles began; the late 1980s and early 90s became a time of political turmoil in the Fishing Section and good relations with the swimming club were sometimes strained. The discovery of some questionable practices in the Fishing Section did not help and, as with the swimming club a decade earlier, a wane set in. This was evidenced not by a fall in membership numbers but by a large turnover of members. The situation was turned around by the appointment of Colin Hannan as Hon. Head Bailiff in 1992. He had became concerned at what was happening amongst the anglers and managed to restore the club's fortunes. The whole ethos changed after 1992 which was also the last year that angling matches were held at Henleaze Lake.

Fish Stocks

1995 was the last year that a mandatory close season had to be observed at the lake. Until that year the Salmon and Freshwater Fisheries Act of 1975 made coarse fishing in the lake illegal for a period of three months every year (midnight on 14 March to midnight on 15 June). Accordingly it had become customary until 1990 to avoid complete closure of the lake for fishing during the close season by the provision of trout fishing. Not that this was a new venture – the club had been stocking the lake with trout every January or February since at least 1950. After 1995 the close season was relaxed because it was finally recognised that the law which was supposed to protect spawning fish was ineffective: spawning occurred outside the close season as well as in it. Since 1996 coarse fishing has taken place at Henleaze Lake the year round except for those few days that the fish are seen to be spawning, when the bailiffs summarily suspend fishing.

Until 1988 no-one knew exactly what fish stocks there were in the lake. It become evident that before the war Major Stanley Badock must have placed some crucian carp in the lake in addition to the trout he put in. Otherwise very little stocking with

Colour Fig. 3.7 A 24 lbs 12 oz pike caught in Henleaze Lake. The pike come even bigger than this and will occasionally nibble at swimmers, especially the small children. (photo Steve Freeman)

Colour Fig. 3.8 The 'barley straw team' at work in February 1998. Every year 'sausages' of loosely packed barley straw are fabricated and placed on the water at the edges of the Henleaze Lake. As the straw rots it releases algaecide which enhances water clarity. Ten bales of barley straw are converted into 20 'sausages' early in spring every year and a further five bales' worth is added to the water during the summer. The process was recommended to us by the secretary of the Country Land Owners Association and the Environment Agency issues a definitive document on its use. (photo Derek Klemperer)

Colour Fig. 3.9 Barley straw 'sausages' are distributed around the lake perimeter to counter algal growth and improve water quality. (photo Derek Klemperer)

Colour Fig. 3.10 The voracious yellow lilies are kept in check by physically hauling out the roots. This is a lousy job for the bailiffs, clad in dry suits with substantial boots: the muddy lily roots tend to come out festooned with glass shards, fishing line and rusty tins. (photo Derek Klemperer)

Colour Fig. 3.11 Clearing yellow lilies provides the bailiffs with an opportunity to transplant some of the prettier and less prolific white lilies. (photo Derek Klemperer)

Colour Fig. 3.12 A 64 square metre floating island bearing a variety of pre-planted water plants is being towed into position on 11 July 2006. In the background there is a similar floating island that was assembled and placed in position on 10 April 2005. Note the growth that has taken place over the intervening 13 months. Hinged attachments to the cliff wall allow these islands to float up and down with fluctuating water level. The modular construction by Water-Lines Solutions enables any size of island to be assembled. The plants take nutrient from the water hydroponically and discourage the growth of algae. The roots also provide shelter from predators for the smaller fish. (photo Jonathan Sturt)

Colour Fig. 3.13 Henleaze Lake flood water covered most of the car park after heavy rains in December 1992. The pump broke down and had to be replaced before the water level could be brought under control. No pumping had been needed during the previous two winters. Our picture shows the then Club President inspecting the picturesque situation. (photo Derek Klemperer)

Colour Fig. 4.1 An angler member contentedly fishing in January 1999. Henleaze anglers are a tough breed, fishing in all weathers and air temperatures with aplomb and many enjoy fishing through the hours of darkness too. Their wives and partners have to be understanding, unless they are in the 3% that fish too. Britain is alleged to have four million anglers, making angling the number one sport in the country. (photo Derek Klemperer)

Colour Fig. 4.2 Photograph taken at the traditional New Year's Day swim at Henleaze Lake, 1 January 2002. 1¹/₄ inch thick ice had to be broken on this occasion so that swimmers could get into the 36.5 °F (2¹/₂ °C) water. The air temperature was –5 °C. The blood circulation was revived with the traditional punch and mince pies for swimmers and cheering watchers alike. (photo Martin Layzell)

Colour Fig. 4.3 Swimmers competing in the 2002 Gloucester County ASA Open Water Championships. The water on this occasion was 18 °C (64 °F). Brrrr. This event has been held annually at Henleaze Lake since 1999. The number of swimmers competing has consistently been between 50 and 60. Both Henleaze Swimming Club and Bristol Henleaze Swimming Club are always well represented. The winners in the various age groups of the 1000 metres (Juniors) and 2000 metres (Seniors) events are awarded certificates and may be selected to compete in national championship events. Some of the swimmers go on to other open water events. (photo Mark Thompson)

Colour Fig. 4.4 Mr Brown's Pig tells magical children's stories to Henleaze Swimming Club juniors during the Millennium Celebration held at the lake on 16 July 2000. There were children's fancy dress prizes, inflatables on the water, a band, some dancing, an exhibition of archival photographs, and a special newsletter. (photo Mervyn Rowles)

Colour Fig. 4.5 At one party held at the lake children were invited to try rowing a genuine coracle. It's not as easy as it looks! (photo Derek Klemperer)

Colour Fig. 4.6 A group of triathlon swimmers in 2006. The Bristol and District Triathlon Club (BADTri), set up in 2004, started training at the lake in 2006 for triathlons and iron man events which involve open water swimming. (photo Mark Thompson)

Colour Fig. 4.7 For the filming of *Nectar* on 14 May 2005 the director Liz Crow and the producer Abigail Davies transformed the entire swimming end of the lake into its 1931 appearance. Walter, the deaf Olympic aspirant, could then be seen competing in the 200 yards men's freestyle trials, just as it looked in that year. The club's 18mm motion film showing Olympic diver Pete Desjardins and swimmers performing at Henleaze Lake in 1935 was an invaluable guide to getting it right. (photo Mark Thompson)

Colour Fig. 4.8 Henleaze Swimming Club members were recruited as extras for the filming of *Nectar*. A comprehensive wardrobe was brought to the lake to attire them with sartorial elegance of the 1930s. (photo Mark Thompson)

Colour Fig. 4.9 A group of swimming club superintendents photographed in August 2004. The superintendents are employed by the club to perform multifarious duties that include checking membership cards, watching over the entrance and operating the barrier, watching duty at the waters side, putting out various equipments at the start of the day and taking them in at closing time, signing in guests, and dealing with enquiries. It can get hectic on a hot sunny day. (photo Mark Thompson)

Colour Fig. 4.10 Some of the Henleaze Swimming Club Executive Committee members pose with the club's championship cups during the Mid-Summers Day event in 2006. (photo Mark Thompson)

Colour Fig. 4.11 Swimmers congregating at the club limit on a hot August afternoon in 1999 when the water temperature was 72 °F (22 °C). Swimming to and from the east cliff where 'club limit' is painted on the cliff face is a popular beat amongst members. It was here that a load of wet concrete descended from the cliff top onto the water where people were swimming one day! (photo Derek Klemperer)

Colour Fig. 4.12 Some rubbish retrieved from the lake floor by Colin Hannan in his dry suit. This picture was taken to confirm the saying 'everything including the kitchen sink'! Regrettably tipping is a feature of everyday life at the lake. Not that Henleaze Lake has been singled out for special treatment – we seem to be a nation of fly tippers. (photo Alan Giles)

Colour Fig. 4.13 A light-hearted moment celebrating the plunge champion's record breaking length achieved during the 2006 Mid-summer Beano at Henleaze Lake. (photo Mark Thompson)

Colour Fig. 4.14 The Gas Works Singers performing at Henleaze Lake during the 2006 Mid-summer Beano. Choirs and bands have often performed at the lake during social events and once during the filming of *Nectar* in 2005. (photo Mark Thompson)

Colour Fig. 4.15 Three girls swimming by the willow tree branches that hang into the water near the club swimming limit. This willow tree is one of the six trees that were given to the club and planted by Dr Stanley Badock in 1938; they all still grace the club grounds. (photo Mark Thompson)

Colour Fig. 4.16 Poster advertising the screening of the film *Nectar*. The film, which depicts events in 1931, was shot at Henleaze Lake and the lake was transformed into an authentic 1931 setting for filming to take place. (poster by Director Liz Crow)

Fig. 3.8 In 1985 the Avon Preservation and Restocking Society netted at least 5000 stunted roach at Henleaze Lake and released them into the River Frome. This was followed in 1988 by a formal survey of fish stocks in the lake by Wessex Water Authority, forerunner, in turn, of the National Rivers Authority and then the Environmental Agency. A balanced stock of a wide variety of coarse fish was subsequently built up often with the help of these bodies. (photo Derek Klemperer)

coarse fish occurred until the 1960s and much of that was wiped out in 1969. During the 1980s various fish were added to the water every year but little thought was given to the overall balance of species. For a while every pike that was caught was unwisely killed. One result of this was that the lake once again became overrun with stunted roach that were unable to grow. At least 5000 of these roach were netted in 1985 (Fig. 3.8) and released into the River Frome at Frenchay. The netting

Fig. 3.9 Most of the water was pumped out of Henleaze Lake in October 1988 so that Wessex Water Authority could make a netting survey of the fish in the lake. The survey established for the first time what fish there were in the lake. The opportunity was also taken to clear away the lily roots shown in the foreground together with masses of rubbish. Springs in the old quarry walls and floor enabled most of the water to return within ten days after pumping ceased and excess water even had to be pumped out of the lake in March 1989. These were the halcyon years before water tables all over the country started to fall. (photo Derek Klemperer)

was carried out by the Avon Preservation and Restocking Society to which Henleaze Fishing Section became affiliated from 1986 until the Society disbanded in 1996. APRS was a farsighted society that was founded in 1908 and only disbanded when its function was effectively taken over first by Wessex Water Authority and eventually by the Environmental Agency.

With a view to recommending a sensible stocking programme, Wessex Water Authority pumped 50 million gallons (being most of the water) out of the lake in October 1988 (Fig. 3.9) and then made a detailed netting survey. The survey report enabled the bailiffs to start a gradual build-up of a large and varied fish stock which has finally made Henleaze Lake one of the best private fishing waters in the West Country.

The lake contains a full range of coarse fish, including tench (Colour Fig. 3.2) and bream (Colour Fig. 3.4) that are both breeding well. Carpers can enjoy fishing for a variety of different carp species with weights in double figures i.e. over 10 lbs. (Colour Fig. 3.6); some carp in the lake weigh over 20 lbs. Anglers have to match their wits against carp, which are hard to catch, and when caught they put up a robust fight. Colour Fig. 3.5 shows an angler 'playing' a carp. Anglers will happily stay overnight hoping to catch the big one which may even be one of those known by name – individuals can be identified from their scales. The standard bivouac tent provides rest and shelter (Colour Fig. 3.3). There are plenty of pike to maintain a natural balance throughout the stock and for the specialist pikers to catch (Colour Fig. 3.7). The lake also contains eels (Fig. 3.10) alleged to have reached the water overland! All fish known to be present in Henleaze Lake are listed in Appendix 2.

Subscribing members of Henleaze Swimming Club's Fishing Section and their guests may cast their lines at the lake during virtually every day or night of the year.

Fig. 3.10 An eel caught in Henleaze Lake. This eel weighed 6 lbs and is about 40 years old. Eels have been known to cross the Atlantic Ocean and are alleged to have reached Henleaze Lake over land! (photo Mervyn Hunt)

During the five summer months May to September they may have a choice of 36 swims beyond the fishing gate and during the seven winter months they may also fish round the swimming end of the lake. They may also fish the waters of the Bristol and West of England Federation of Anglers with which the Henleaze Fishing Section has been affiliated since 1989. The Federation waters include a stretch of the River Avon so that Henleaze anglers can also enjoy river fishing at no extra charge.

In 2005 a comprehensive questionnaire was distributed to all Henleaze anglers in order to ascertain what they felt about all aspects of fishing at the lake. The high return of completed answers was analysed and led to the circulation of a survey report and the formulation of future plans. Today's bailiffs keep things shipshape and Bristol fashion. The anglers know the head bailiff can be their best friend at the lakeside but at the same time he is hard on defaulters. In this atmosphere of bonhomie the anglers are not above pulling his leg.

One time the Head Bailiff found some abandoned lady's clothing on the bank at the far end of the lake. This caused alarm and consternation, a check with the police for missing persons and a search of the water nearby where the clothes had been found. Then a search of the retrieved clothes revealed that they were a very odd assortment – two pairs of Anne Summers' size 42 peep-through brassieres, three pairs of crotchless panties . . . . On another occasion the catch of an enormous cat fish, complete with 9 inch long whiskers was enthusiastically reported by several anglers to the head bailiff. There are still anglers about who will tell you who caught it and what it looked like at the weigh-in but no photo of the fish was taken. The bailiffs can always get their own back by announcing that the carp are to be culled because there are far too many in the lake . . . .

The Quality of the Lake Water

Since the swimming club's formation the water in the lake has been subjected to regular independent analysis to ensure its purity and suitability for swimming and diving. The earliest detailed analyses to survive date from 1938. The analysis reports continue throughout the war and run right up to modern times. In August 1947 the city's Medical Officer of Health decided that he should take his own weekly samples of lake water for analysis in addition to the analyses that were being carried out for the club by the private firm of Cook and Barke at the Western Counties Laboratory.

This led to a spirited exchange of letters between the Bristol City and County Department of Public Health, the club's Hon. Secretary Laurie McGowan, and the water analysts Cook and Barke who had regularly tested the lake water and declared it to be OK for bathing. In a letter dated 11th October 1947 the city's Chief Sanitary Inspector wrote 'the lake is potentially dangerous for bathing purposes and it would be advisable that chlorination be implemented'. As a result the lake was chlorinated straight away in the manner instructed by the city's Chlorination Officer using chloros, which is a weak aqueous solution of calcium hypochlorite. Only a few days later, on 16 October, Harold Barke, the club's analyst expressed a dim view of chlorination, adding that 'our only chance of escape, as far as I can see, is to consult a biologist'. Furthermore 'the whole thing is a bounce on the part of the Authority, who know nothing of the purification of a lake as distinct from a bath'. The club Hon. Secretary agreed, writing 'I feel very strongly that we ought now to start fighting any interference on the part of the local authorities' and 'that their authority does not go beyond the public swimming baths'; furthermore they have 'no right to enter private premises'.

The battle continued during the swimming close season with the analyst pointing out to the city's Medical Officer of Health that chlorination was objectionable because of

'1. The great volume of water to be dealt with, and the difficulties of mixing.
2. The self purification of the water.
3. The fact that I [the club's analyst] watch over the condition of the water.
4. That the entry to the lake is private.'

This did not have the desired effect. A later letter from the analyst to the club's Hon. Secretary states: 'I regret to learn that the Medical Officer of Health is still plaguing you. I am satisfied that they have found no evidence of pollution in the water, beyond a few *Faecal Coli* per 100 cubic centimetres. These occur in all exposed waters, including say Blagdon and Cheddar Lakes.'

Despite the analyst's opposition, diluted chloros was sprayed onto the lake and poured over the banks on and off until at least 1982 to counter any possibility of infection occasioned by rodents. The futility of the treatment, not to mention its detrimental effect on fish, was finally recognised by the authorities who came up with a welcome change of heart in 1982. The Wessex Water Authority, as it was then, formally complained to the club that chlorination was illegal and that the practice had to stop and henceforth chloros was only officially used in the toilet block. Nevertheless Dr C.V. James, the club's analyst from the 1960s until his death in 1988, actually recommended chlorination.

In 1983, analysis of the water was put onto a more formal basis of once a month and costs for these tests first appear in the accounts for 1984. Dr C.V. James of Cook and Barke was a swimming member and a personal friend of the club's Hon. Treasurer Bob Steel. When he died in 1988 the Western Counties Laboratory closed and analysis was taken over by the Public Health Laboratory in Bristol. Samples were taken at the same time at various locations around the lake. These tests are essentially an *Escherichia Coli* count and samples are now normally taken every fortnight during the summer.

The frequency of testing is increased in very hot weather: the temperature of lake water topped 25 °C (77 °F) in 1995 and reached 24.4 °C (76 °F) in 2003. The water quality is consistently acceptable for swimmers and fish alike although it cannot match the quality of sea water at coastal beaches (at least those that do not have a sewage outflow nearby). It will never, of course, match chlorinated swimming pools.

Occasionally skin irritations have been reported by persons with sensitive skin. One cause of this irritation is thought to be the condition known as 'swimmers itch'; it is a temporary allergic reaction acquired by susceptible bathers who come into contact with tiny worms called *miracidia*. The worms originate from infected water fowl, snails, and mammals whose faecal material contains the worm eggs. Several hours after leaving the water the swimmer experiences a distinct itch. Swimmers itch has good coverage on the internet; the best defence for swimmers could be to towel down vigorously immediately on leaving the water and before the water evaporates. We first heard about 'swimmer's itch' from the manager of Keynes Country Park, which is Bristol's nearest open water swimming available to the public.

Algal growth in the lake water is treated by placing barley straw into the water in March, when the water starts to warm up, and again in July as a booster. Barley straw has the unique property of releasing vastly more algaecide as it rots than anything else; the algaecide that is released has been shown to be hydrogen peroxide. Being an aerobic process the barley straw requires both air and water to act so the straw is fluffed up and loosely packed into Christmas tree netting sleeves using a netting machine (Colour Fig. 3.8). The loosely packed 'sausages' are kept afloat by interspersing the straw filling with sealed plastic bottles. The sausages are then towed out by boat and anchored around the perimeter of the lake (Colour Fig. 3.9). Started at Henleaze Lake in 1998, the annual exercise has achieved good results in terms of water clarity. The cost is minimal and there is no danger of deleterious environmental impact such as treatment with chemicals might occasion.

Discovered by chance, the process is now recommended by the Environment Agency which issues a detailed paper on the subject. Barley straw is widely used in inland waters and reservoirs, notably in Rutland Water, a large reservoir in Leicestershire that is stocked with trout which must have a clear view to feed.

Another 'natural' water clarification process involves the use of a finely-divided porous mineral limestone of marine origin trade named Aquaplankton. This product is sold in pet shops for use in garden ponds but it turned out to be prohibitively expensive to treat a water the size of Henleaze Lake. A cheaper mineral limestone product named Siltex appears to be the same as Aquaplankton. It was used on the lake in conjunction with barley straw for the first time in March 2006. Easy to apply, it is simply spread all over the lake surface. In addition to ostensibly helping to clarify the water, Siltex is claimed to aid the digestion of organic sludge that can accumulate at the bottom of deep waters, especially those that are subject to stratification.

Various other water treatments have been used at Henleaze Lake. At one time the water was clarified by towing a porous bag of copper sulphate behind a boat. Permanganate of potash has also been used. As with chloros, these chemical treatments were clearly not popular and they were, of course, poisonous for fish stocks, especially the small fry. By the same token it is salutary to observe here that fish die if they are placed in domestic tap water – one could not therefore top up the lake from the water main! We should add here that the voracious yellow water lilies growing in the lake were once poisoned with a selective herbicide. However nowadays the bailiffs, clad in dry suits and boots, keep the lily pads in check by pulling out the roots in autumn when the water level is at its lowest (Colour Fig. 3.10). This is a rotten job and physically very demanding. It provides an opportunity to transplant some of the more attractive but slower growing white lilies (Colour Fig. 3.11).

The long hot summer of 1976 was blighted when a boy who had spent many days swimming at the lake contracted *leptospirosis* commonly called Weil's disease. This is an infection of the blood which can be contracted from swimming in water contaminated with rodent's urine. The boy was admitted to hospital and swimming and fishing activities at the lake were banned for a fortnight. Exhaustive tests carried out by the Environmental Health Department failed to demonstrate the presence of any organism in the *leptospira* group and a detailed ecological survey of the lake did not show any of the common animal hosts in the immediate environment of the lake.

Recommendations from the Environmental Health Department were to consider the provision of showers, to keep litter to a minimum, and to make arrangements for more regular routine water purity sampling. The club's finances were not good at this time but cold showers were finally installed in 1981; they were upgraded to hot showers in 1999, the year of the club's 80th birthday (81st season).

Further adverse publicity occurred in the hot summer of 1984 when another 16-year-old boy who had been swimming in the lake became infected with *leptospirosis*. A notice dated 1st August 1984 was served on John White the club's Hon. Secretary which required 'steps to be taken to destroy rats or mice or to keep land free from rats and mice on the land known as Henleaze Lake, and to provide on the land sufficient rodenticide to control the infestation'. A press release was issued by the Environmental Health Department and the lake was closed for just over two weeks.

By mid-August the level of the water had risen 30 cm and no evidence of the bacterium responsible for *leptospirosis* had been found. In spite of this, the health department decided that the lake water was not good and left the club to take the decision to reopen the lake for swimming. The club's installation of poison bait boxes, regularly serviced by an outside contractor dates from this time.

The two *leptospirosis* scares were made more damaging for the club by the media which announced that a club member had contracted the disease in 1976 and again in 1984 but did not subsequently report that on each occasion lake water was cleared as the source of infection. We have already mentioned a malaise in the swimming club's fortunes that began in the 1960s and the *leptospirosis* scares undoubtedly contributed to the club's further decline at the time they occurred.

In more recent times there has been a growing awareness that a programme of planting water-edge plants suited to the lake would be beneficial for the quality of the water. Water plants take the nutrient out of the water that would otherwise be available for algae to grow. The problem of fluctuating water levels can be overcome by putting a variety of emergent plants suitable for hydroponic growth onto floating islands. The floor of these islands consists of coir roll, allowing the plant roots to dangle 1 or 2 metres down into the water. As a bonus, the roots provide safe haven for small fish which need to escape from predators such as pike or cormorants. Colour Fig. 3.12 shows pre-planted floating islands that were assembled at Henleaze Lake in 2005 and 2006. Such islands supplement the beneficial effect of putting barley straw into the water. Club officers have also taken advice on the introduction of free-floating water plants such as hornwort. The Lake Management Committee oversees these developments and is active in planning, planting, and caring for the lake water, the banks and the land areas. Generous grants from the Environment Agency for habitat improvement were secured in 2005 and 2006. All the water flora to be found at Henleaze Lake are listed in Appendix 2.

The Lake Water Level

No-one knows the exact hydrology of Henleaze Lake, although being situated in limestone country that is full of cracks and fissures the lake must be in connection with other waters in the area, albeit with very long time constants. There is no natural surface outflow of water from the lake and inflow occurs via a number of springs below the water level. Dye tests have failed to prove a connection with Pen Park Hole, the huge local cavern in which the water level is known to fluctuate by over 15 metres (50 feet). The cavern is situated 1.4 crow km (0.9 miles) from the northern end of Henleaze Lake and why there should be such a large water level fluctuation in it or where the water comes from has never been explained.

It is also not known whether the water level in Henleaze Lake is affected by any abstraction from the two bore holes situated at the Airbus works in Filton (formerly British Aerospace) and at Filton golf course. The bore hole at the Airbus works is 2.6 crow km (1.6 miles) from Henleaze Lake. It was sunk to serve as a war time emergency source of water and is still used from time to time to abstract water from the aquifer. A two-year licence was granted in 1984, for instance, permitting a maximum of 82 cubic metres to be pumped in any one day. Pumping was not allowed if the water level in Henleaze Lake fell below the entrance to the club's outflow pipe, as ascertained by weekly inspections.

In 1991 a 120 metre (394 feet) deep bore hole was sunk at Filton golf course 1.9 crow km (1.2 miles) from Henleaze Lake and an abstraction licence was sought by the golf club. The purpose of this bore hole was to provide water for two ponds which would then be used to water the fairways as needed. It is sobering to recall that Tony Elliott, the swimming club's Hon. Solicitor (and Hon. Life Member) was working at his desk the day after the Notice of Application for a Licence to Abstract was published but died two days later.

At a meeting with the National Rivers Authority's Abstraction Licensing Officer in 1992 Henleaze Swimming Club's officers succeeded in ensuring that abstraction from the Filton Golf Club's borehole would only be allowed between 1 January and 31 March in any year and then only 'during the times when there is excess water in the ground water system'. In order to conform to the terms of the abstraction licence that was issued, the Filton Golf Club manager holds a key to the gate of Henleaze Lake so that the water level in the lake with respect to the outflow pipe for excess water can be monitored. In 1997 an application by Filton Golf Club to abstract water during the summer months was refused after revived discussions. The bottom line which one has always to bear in mind is that Filton Golf Club can exist without water whereas Henleaze Swimming Club cannot.

There being neither a visible inflow nor a surface outflow, Henleaze Lake is basically just a scenic man-made hole that has flooded. Nevertheless swimmers will sometimes notice an up-welling of colder water from the springs that exist below the water level. There has never been any connection with the Hen stream that runs under Lake Road by the gate to Henleaze Lake. This stream, which rises in Horfield has now been culverted through to the west side of Southmead Road where it emerges into the daylight in the former garden of The Manor House. It then flows through the old garden, under Lake Road, beside Willowbank Flats, and on to join the River Trym in Badock Woods (cp Fig. 1.5 in Chapter 1 showing the 1936 Ordnance Survey map of the area). In the former Manor House garden, once the property of the Badock family, the Hen stream flows past a ruined seventeenth-century summer house (Fig. 3.11). This Grade II listed ruin is situated 100 metres from the gate to Henleaze Lake.

The culvert taking the Hen stream under Lake Road is only a couple of metres from the gate to Henleaze Lake and from where the entrance drive slopes down. Fig. 1.7 in Chapter 1 clearly shows a dam that used to exist at the southern end of Southmead Quarry (now Henleaze Lake). This dam was probably built to avoid the Hen stream pouring into the quarry workings at times of flood. In more recent times the authorities had to widen the culvert to avoid the occasional flooding of Glenwood Road back gardens. The Hen stream has given its name to Henleaze which means the meadow by the Hen. It is unlikely that Henleaze is a corruption of Henleys, Henley being the name of a once prominent family in the area; their name is perpetuated in Henley Grove.

During the winter months the lake sometimes floods naturally and we have referred elsewhere to the necessity of pumping down the water level to keep the

Fig. 3.11 The ruined seventeenth-century summer house in the former garden of The Manor House. This Grade II listed building stands by a stream in an isolated piece of wooded land bounded on all sides by private property. You can spot it between the bungalows in Lake Road opposite the gate to Henleaze Lake. The ruin must have been familiar to the Badock family during their one-time residency in The Manor House. (photo Derek Klemperer)

water from rising over the lawns and the car park. Fig. 3.12 shows how the lake flooded one winter in the 1940s. To obviate the flooding problem, which in the past sometimes delayed opening for the swimming season, a permanent pump was installed in 1969. The pump draws water from a concrete sump that is fed by a 23 cm (9 inch) diameter drain (outflow pipe) opening onto the water take-off port which is situated at the south west corner of the lake. Water flows into the sump whenever the water level in the lake rises above the lip of the take-off port. Water that collects in the sump may then be pumped out to the main sewer under the far side of Lakewood Road opposite the Willowbank flats. The system works well except for the astonishing number of frogs that manage to traverse the 62 metre (204 feet) long drain pipe and end up trapped in the sump. It is interesting to note here that current wisdom at the time of construction asserted that pumping down the water level would not work because one would be pumping against the water table prevailing in the district.

On the other hand, after the lake water level had been pumped right down by Wessex Water Authority in October 1988 (to make a survey of fish stocks possible) the water level rebounded fully in ten days. While the lake was almost empty at least four springs were observed bubbling in the old quarry floor. One of them is shown in Fig. 3.13. There is also a spring which rises occasionally from the east cliff face (Lake Road side) above the high water mark. Mossy patches and chalky deposits

Fig. 3.12 Henleaze Lake is shown flooded in the 1940s. This used to be quite usual in winter time and it occasionally delayed the opening of the swimming season. A permanent pump was installed in 1969 to lower the water level and obviate this situation. (Doug Satherley collection)

Fig. 3.13 The spring which issues from the old quarry floor at the foot of the diving tower. This photograph was taken looking straight down from the concreted bank after Wessex Water Authority had pumped most of the water out of the lake in October 1988 for the purpose of conducting a survey of the fish stock. (photo Derek Klemperer)

Fig. 3.14 *Left:* The spring which issues into Henleaze Lake near to where 'Club Limit' is now painted on the cliff face froze solid in about 1947, when this picture was taken. You can see it as a white patch on the cliff face above the frozen lake water level to the right of the raft. The lake is evidently flooded because the little willow tree at the right hand side has wet feet. *Right:* Detail of the frozen spring. Situated well above the high water mark, this spring is less active nowadays, as indeed are other springs on the old quarry floor. This reflects a general trend towards lower water levels throughout the country. (Doug Satherley collection)

give its location away about ten metres to the south of where 'Club Limit' is painted on the cliff. (Fig. 3.14 left and right). The exposure of these springs during quarrying must have been a contributory factor in ending the extraction of limestone in 1912.

In accordance with Murphy's Law (also known as Sod's law) the pump broke down irreparably just as severe flooding occurred in December 1992. This flooding is documented in Colour Fig. 3.13. A modern self-priming pump was bought from and installed by Sterne (Fluid Engineering) Ltd., and the situation was saved. This pump is capable of lowering the lake water level 8 cm (3 inches) in 24 hours. Since the 1990s flooding has become less frequent and pumping has not been necessary every winter, and none since the winter of 2001/2002. The opposite concern to flooding now engages the Executive Committee's attention because the lake water has fallen to alarmingly low levels on several occasions. With low water tables throughout the land and some rivers losing their water altogether, low water is clearly nothing peculiar to Henleaze Lake. We have, however, had to pump in 2007!

CHAPTER 4
ACTIVITIES AND RUNNING THE CLUB

carpe diem

Activities at the Lake

In recent years there have been some 1350 swimming members, 200 angling members, a hard working Executive Committee, a well maintained lake property, and a calendar of organised events. Unlike the anglers who are at the lake throughout the year (Colour Fig. 4.1), the official swimming season with superin-tendents on duty every day only spans the five summer months. Nevertheless working parties are invited to swim off their sweat from October to April and there is, of course, the New Year's Day swim (Colour Fig. 4.2) which event reached its eighth successive year in 2006.

Older traditions that suffered a lacuna have been revived. The lake gala days of yore are now taking place at the lake as the Gloucester County Amateur Swimming Association's Open Water Championships. These one day events have been brought to the lake annually since 1999 through the efforts of Alan Giles, the Chairman of the swimming club's Executive Committee from 1992 onwards and more recently the ASA's Open Water Secretary. Swimmers in these events compete under ASA laws and technical rules over a 2000 metre course at the lake, reduced to 1000 metres for juniors (Colour Fig. 4.3). National ASA officials who are present in these county events select the best swimmers who go on to compete in the national cham-pionships held elsewhere.

As mentioned in Chapter 2, early morning swimming was reintroduced at the lake after a lapse of 47 years. In 2004, the first year it was tried, 14 Friday morning openings at 7.15 a.m. attracted an average of 12 swimmers. Since 1995 the committee has organised two or three 'long swims' (Fig. 4.1). At these heavily attended fun swims all members, especially juniors, are invited to swim the 220 metres (0.137 miles) length of the lake as far as the flag which is planted on the rocky point way down in the fishing area. Swimmers are also invited, of course, to swim back although exit places are arranged at strategic points on the banks. But many of the participants 'bag' one mile by swimming there and back again four times. In 2002 Lee Portingale, the then head coach of Bristol Henleaze Swimming Club set the pace by swimming 17 double lengths, a total of 7480 metres (4.65 miles). He only came out of the water because there was no more time left before general swimming resumed.

Lee's training regime also showed in the BHSC Channel relay swim which he led with his brother in 2004. Until he moved from Bristol to Hitchin Swimming Club in London at the end of 2005, Lee could be seen lapping the lake for two or three

Fig. 4.1 Swimmers in one of the 1999 'Long Swims' have just reached their furthest point up the lake and are turning round. They now head back to the distant starting board. Swimmers are started at half hourly intervals for this annual fun swim which takes swimmers half way down the lake into the angling area – and back. 'Long Swims' are held a couple of times each swimming season and certificates of achievement giving the distance covered are signed by the president and awarded to swimmers. These certificates are much coveted by junior club members. Until 2005 they were facsimile reproductions of the original 1933 Endurance Test Certificate which is illustrated in Fig. 4.13 near the end of this chapter. (photo Derek Klemperer)

hours several times a week, even when the water temperature was below 60 °F (16 °C). The authors once watched him swim 4 km in an hour when the lake water temperature was 52 °F (11 °C). Amazingly, his last lap always takes exactly the same time as his first.

Diving learner classes have also taken place in recent times but with a paid coach, there being no position of Hon. Diving Coach as in former times. Nevertheless exhibition platform diving could still be seen at Henleaze Lake as recently as 2005, when the club's high diver and gymnast Ron Smith frequently showed off his skills before admiring onlookers (Fig. 4.2). In 2006 Ron moved away from Bristol.

At the end of every swimming season there is the traditional 'Last Swim Together' event with attendant conviviality and refreshments. Swimmers are entered for a prize draw which takes place at the club's AGM at the end of November. AGMs are enlivened by showing a short film or pictures taken at the lake; sometimes an invited speaker will give a talk on a swimming or a fishing subject. Thereafter AGMs end with a mixer and refreshments.

The Executive Committee also organises a number of social functions for members. Special events were held for the club's 80th birthday on 18th July 1999,

Fig. 4.2 Club member Ron Smith displays his diving skill from the 7 metre high platform at Henleaze Lake in 2005. The 10 metre platform at the top of the picture was disabled in 1991 after the Health and Safety Executive recommended minimum depths of water at plummet. Ron, who is also a gymnast, has been an Olympic diving judge. Diving, both as a participant and as a spectator sport, has always been enjoyed at Henleaze Lake. (photo Ken Mitchell)

the new millennium celebration on 16th July 2000 (one event is shown in Colour Fig. 4.4), and the Golden Jubilee on 3rd June 2002. Annually, on the June Saturday nearest to the summer solstice, there is a Midsummer Party with the lake grounds staying open until 9 p.m. Competition plunging was started in 2004 as a fun event during this social gathering. In 2006 the winning plunge measured 17.34 metres. Colour Fig. 4.13 shows the jubilant plunge champion making the most of it. Hot and cold drinks are laid on in the marquee, there may be a barbecue, a band, or a choir (Colour Fig. 4.14), and there may be some dancing (reminiscent of those latter day flannel dances?) whilst juniors enjoy games, all in the atmosphere that the lake environment encourages. One year the children were invited to try handling a genuine coracle on the lake (Colour Fig. 4.5). Occasional American suppers are also held at the lake during the summer.

On busy days in the season an outside contractor sells refreshments to members and their guests. At other times members can make their own tea and toast using the club room facilities. Members guests (who must be able to swim) are always welcome at the lake. They provide a significant proportion of club revenue. Health and Safety considerations and ruling by the club's insurers obviate letting people off the street into the lake premises. Gone are the pre-war days when members of the public could enter the premises by simply paying 6d (6 old pence equal to $2^1/2$ new pence).

The lake facility is, nevertheless, often made available to outside bodies for their organised activities. A number of groups train in the lake; a local life-saving group,

84

Fig. 4.3 Scuba divers are searching the lake floor as part of the Bristol Diving School's training session at Henleaze Lake in November 1997. The divers have to retrieve heavy objects using air bags after the instructor has thrown them in. This is not a cheap sport because the equipment costs £2,000 for each diver. (photo Derek Klemperer)

police divers and scuba diving clubs (Fig. 4.3) and the Bristol and District Triathletes (BADTri) (Colour Fig. 4.6). In the 1960s the celebrated Dr Oliver C. Lloyd regularly brought his team of dedicated cave divers to train in the lake for 3 / 6d per head per visit. They especially appreciated the dark, cold and murky depths the lake offers. Schools have used the lake for canoeing instruction (Fig. 4.4 left) and both scouts and a scheme for unemployed youths have used the lake for practical raft construction (Fig. 4.4 right).

In 1989 Forum Television shot scenes at the lake for the film *I likes me music* which is about the young people living in the Southmead area of Bristol. Amongst other film units the BBC and HTV have used the lake on several occasions; filming for the BBC's *Casualty* series in 1993 (Fig. 4.5) involved the creation of a sham lock gate, complete with make-believe algae-covered surfaces and in 2005 film director Liz Crow and producer Abigail Davies used the lake as a location for the film *Nectar* about a deaf champion swimmer. For this film the lake was completely transformed into its 1930s appearance (Colour Figs. 4.7 and 4.16). A large number of club members were recruited as extras to perform as spectators in the film, all suitably dressed in 1930s clothes (Colour Fig. 4.8).

Fishing facilities were made available for youngsters during their school holidays through the police SPLASH (School Police Liaison Activities during the School Holidays) programme in 1987, 1988 and 1989. A joint scheme run by the police and

Fig. 4.4 *Left:* Clifton College Combined Cadet Force being trained in the art of safe canoeing at Henleaze Lake. This photograph, taken on 10 November 1997, appeared in the college magazine. Many other local Bristol schools have made use of the lake for canoe training.

Right: The 38th Bristol Scout Group constructed and successfully sailed rafts on Henleaze Lake in July 2001. Raft construction teaches one a lot about buoyancy, load bearing, team work, and, of course, knot tying. (photos Derek Klemperer)

Henbury Park/Blaise Castle Estate rangers held a fishing workshop at the lake in 1999 and again in 2000. The fire brigade practise using their hoses with lake water; this helps to aerate the water, which is especially welcome in hot weather when the solubility of life-giving oxygen is low and the club's electric aerator has to work overtime (Fig. 4.6)

Local school pupils have been granted access to the lake to pursue an area project and, on another occasion, as one of their venues during the School Enrichment Week. In 1986 the Avon Bat Group conducted a bat survey and other wildlife groups have been permitted to carry out surveys on owls and on foxes. Not that such surveys are always benign: in 1990 a fox catcher worked at the lake using free-running snares and cages baited with wild duck with the express purpose of catching and shooting foxes. The animals known to be living on the Henleaze Lake property are listed in Appendix 2.

Rats have also been shot at the lake in the 1980s, notably by John Lawson, the Hon. Head Bailiff for three years (1984–86) and Major John H. Giddings who was on the executive committee for 12 years (1978–89) and Hon. Assistant Treasurer for much of that time. John Giddings' son Keith still has the Webley Tempest .22 air pistol his father used to shoot rats and crows at the lake. (Our crows are notorious for taking the baby ducklings.) But with a breeding cycle of six weeks it is, of course, impossible to eliminate rats entirely from the land.

John Giddings is one of those legendary characters who survived the war against all the odds. Taken prisoner by the Japanese army at the fall of Singapore in February 1942 he spent the next four years in their captivity. He was forced to work on the notorious Burma railway and survived both the slave labour and a whole string of serious tropical diseases without medication. It is hardly surprising that he

Fig. 4.5 Filming for BBC's *Casualty* programme took place at Henleaze Lake on 26 August 1993. This photograph shows the make-believe lock gate that was constructed for a drowning sequence. The BBC has used the lake for filming several times. (photo Derek Klemperer)

was left with a deep hatred for anything Japanese until the day he died in 1996 aged 86.

In May 2006 the club launched its web site at www.henleazeswimmingclub.org. This site covers the history, organisation, and activities of Henleaze Swimming Club and of the Fishing Section and provides useful information and updates for swimming and fishing members and any other interested parties. As at 2006 about 40% of both the swimming and the fishing membership have e-mail addresses,

Fig. 4.6 The club's electric aerator produces a decorative fountain on the water and ensures that the level of dissolved oxygen does not fall to low levels. This is especially important in hot weather when the solubility of oxygen is low anyway. Poor oxygen levels can stress fish and encourage the growth of algae. (photo Derek Klemperer)

indicating that computer ownership is already sufficiently widespread for an interactive web site to be well used. Bristol Henleaze Swimming Club were quicker off the mark: www.bristolhenleazesc.org.uk went online in September 2003.

The Superintendents

Once upon a time the club employed just one man to perform all the duties that fell to the superintendent's lot. The duties included mowing the grass, cutting the hedge, making tea, and servicing the Elsan chemical toilet in the gentlemen's changing lean-to as well as manning the gate. In fact the superintendent saw to everything by himself and could be occupied for all the time he was at the lake. Elsewhere we have mentioned Archie Macfarlane, Sergeant Fred Beaumont, and Dave Prowse, all superintendents who served the club effectively during the 'one-man' period. To these names could be added E.J. Norman, who succeeded the sergeant and was at the lake every day during the season from before opening time until 9 p.m. And many older swimmers will remember Mr Britten whose faithful dog was much feared by intruders. Not all superintendents have been so assiduous in their devotion to club duties; as we have mentioned in Chapter 2, at least one superintendent in the past was relieved of his duties by common accord.

Fig. 4.7 The Lake Road entrance to Henleaze Swimming Club in 1946. There was neither a fence nor a padlocked gate on the club's Lake Road boundary until 1950. The only entrance gate was a low slung structure by the superintendent's hut where the swing bar now stands. Club revellers would sometimes take a midnight swim in those free and easy days. (Doug Satherley collection)

Until 1950 the entrance to the lake consisted of a low gate situated by the super-intendents' hut where the swing bar now stands. There was no padlocked gate on Lake Road for the superintendents to unlock when they came on duty and indeed there was no fence at all on the Lake Road boundary to the club property, just the aforementioned hedge, as shown in Fig. 4.7. A measure of how free and easy it was in the post-war years is afforded by one old timer who told us that it was not unusual for a party to pile into a car following a club dance at St Peter's church hall, drive to the lake, and swim at midnight using the car headlights. Many a fun pastime like this used to be enjoyed that would nowadays make a Health and Safety officer's eyes come out like organ stops.

That is all a distant memory. Nowadays the club employs some dozen superin-tendents who work a roster with two or three on duty at any one time during opening times. Their pay constitutes the largest single item of club expenditure. The longest serving superintendent is Mervyn Rowles; he is well known and liked by successive waves of growing-up members, many of whom he has taught to swim. Mervyn Rowles is third from the left in Colour Fig. 4.9 which shows a group of happy superintendents in their club shirts. Today's superintendent wears a T-shirt that is distinctively coloured in the club's blue or yellow and is embossed with the club crest and name. He or she wears a pin-on name label and carries a walkie talkie for communicating with colleagues in different locations on the property. A windproof jacket is provided for those cooler days when the air heaters in the hut are on too. And there is a handy toaster and microwave oven provided to use at tea time.

Superintendents do a lot more than open the gate and display the water temperature every day. They put out the boat, the safety equipment and the bins before opening and they tidy up after closing time, check swimming and angling members entering the gate, see to the signing-in of visitors (who, as we have said, are a significant source of club income) and there is always one on duty at the lakeside watching over the swimmers and divers. They will close the higher diving stages if the water level falls to below a fiduciary mark. Matters of housekeeping and discipline amongst members are dealt with. They deal with any confrontations, in a professional manner – for instance, when young mums find that they are not allowed to bring their babies in, when the use of a fraudulent membership card is detected or when they find out that a non-member has been smuggled in by hiding in the boot of a car. The existence of stowaway smuggling even brought about the facetious suggestion that superintendents should have mirrors on wheels that could be rolled under cars at the entrance barrier in the same way as was done at Checkpoint Charlie in the days of the Berlin wall.

Fig. 4.8 Superintendents regularly attend first aid and life support training sessions. This picture was taken during an *alfresco* first aid course in June 2001. The dummies are being used to practise mouth-to-mouth resuscitation. (photo Derek Klemperer)

Probably the most important single rule the club has is 'that every member shall have passed a 50 yard swimming test'. Being a deep former quarry there is nowhere that one can stand in the water, the water can be cold and cloudy, quite unlike a heated indoor pool, and the bottom reaches are also dark. To ensure that every applicant for club membership can swim 50 yards in the lake he or she *must* pass this swimming test, watched over by superintendents. Superintendents all attend first aid and basic life support courses (Fig. 4.8), many are qualified life savers and some have attended Risk Assessment and Health and Safety courses. The club, as employer, pays for all courses.

Property Maintenance and Capital Works

It is frequently not realised by members that the club's Executive Committee constitutes an entirely voluntary force which is very active throughout the year and not just in the summer months. Committee members meet every month; they are all honorary and no club employee has been permitted to serve as a committee member since the 2004 elections. This now ensures that committee members cannot run the club for personal gain and obviates the possibility of problems that have notoriously plagued large companies and major construction projects, even at the national level. Historically there have been three superintendents (paid club employees) who were elected to serve on the committee.

Fig. 4.9 The gentlemen's changing lean-to is a rather more basic facility than the ladies changing quarters shown in Fig. 1.18 in Chapter 1 but it has the advantage of being a sheltered suntrap beloved of naturist sunbathers. Unchanged in design since the 1920s, the corrugated iron roof and its supports have been replaced a number of times. This picture was taken in 2002. (photo Joyce Klemperer)

Fig. 4.10 A contractor resurfaces one of the anglers' boardwalks with Keruing hardwood at the northern end of the lake. The platforms that stick out are fishing swims (places for anglers to set up and fish from), one being shown with the steps that will give access to the water whatever the water level. These steps enable the fish anglers catch to be returned gently into the water. (photo Derek Klemperer)

The winter months provide the committee with a respite to deal with major maintenance tasks such as reroofing and refurbishing club buildings without inconveniencing the swimming membership. Fig. 4.9 shows the gentlemen's changing facility, unchanged since the 1920s with the exception of the the roof and the supports being replaced from time to time.

Recurrent projects that the committee addresses include the maintenance, improvement or replacement of the water banks and entry steps, the fences surrounding the property, the diving tower and the diving boards. Attention is given to the safety and rescue equipment, the flower beds and the many trees on the club premises, including those on the top of the cliffs. The various tree species that exist on the club property are listed in Appendix 2. The angling boardwalks have to be maintained in a safe condition (Fig. 4.10) and swims (places to fish) are built into the banks with steps down to the water for the gentle return to the water of fish that have been landed. Angling rules state that all fish are returned to the water in good condition. These steps also provide emergency exits for swimmers during the occasional fun swims that the committee organises into the angling part of the lake.

Typical tasks the committee has managed since 2000 include a new high security fence on the Lake Road frontage, a patio laid out in front of the toilet block, and a new steel storage building behind the ladies' changing rooms for the sit-on grass mowing machine and other equipment. An electric water aerator and a water pressure cleaner have been added to the equipment and power can be supplied via a new heavy duty extension flex that will comfortably reach the ladies' changing rooms for vacuum cleaning or the lakeside for the tea urn. In 2003 the old starting board at the southern end of the lake was replaced by a floating pontoon shown in Colour Fig. 2.2.

The autumn months are a time when lower water levels enable rubbish to be dredged from the lake. It is astonishing to see what can be brought up in addition to the ubiquitous tins and bottles (Colour Fig. 4.12). Local scuba divers practising their skills (cp Fig. 4.3) have brought up a gold watch (not working), a pistol (unloaded), and an enormous pair of steel bolt cutters. Some of the larger rubbish that is reported by swimmers who have made its contact, can be brought to the surface using the bailiff's boat. In this way a road worker's tent frame (with the prongs pointing up) was retrieved. As long ago as 1934 a complete double bed was actually exposed on the lake floor when the lake dried up. What do you make of that, dear reader?

Regrettably, tipping has always been a problem at the lake. On one occasion excess wet concrete was actually discharged over the cliff top onto swimmers below in the club limit area which is shown being enjoyed on a less hazardous day in Colour Figs. 4.11 and 4.15. Once a carpet was lodged above the water half-way down the east cliff for a while and on another occasion anglers were startled by a big splash as a bathroom bath landed in the water and proceeded to sink in stately fashion (the plug must have been left out). Discarded Christmas trees sometimes appear as late as March. On New Year's Day 2006 a 27 inch television set was found floating below the diving tower. One may well ask how on earth it got there.

One day in 1996 the authors' youngest son dived from the 10 metre platform and remained submerged for long enough to start causing anxiety amongst the onlookers. He finally surfaced clutching an old lead accumulator car battery. He dumped the battery on the water edge with the comment that he had found it in the sludge that accumulates in the deep water pit below the diving tower. One wonders what else lies in the pit – perhaps one of the bicycles that was ridden off the top stage in the 1930s? Incidentally, the sludge is not static; springboard and platform divers tend to stir it up when the water level is low. Objects that were tipped over the east cliff face in 2005 included a 3 metre long steel rail that was sticking up in the water. Rusty iron pieces, some steel netting, and shattered bits of pottery were found on the lawns by the diving tower. But the *pièce de résistance* was the stone slab that was dropped into the Hon. Head Bailiff's boat, damaging it. The bailiff could have been killed if he had been in the boat.

Tippers can often be identified and effectively confronted by committee members rather than apprising the environmental authorities who find they can make little progress. More benignly a one-time party in a newly constructed bower on the cliff top (on club land) resulted in paper cups and plates appearing in the lake but more usually it is builder's refuse and garden rubbish that gets tipped as an easy alternative to hiring an expensive skip. The bottom line is always that the club clears up the mess and keeps the property clean. Over the years letters have been circulated to the numerous residents whose gardens back onto the lake property. These bleats only have a limited and temporary effect on the problem.

Other more administrative tasks that occupy committee members include the assembly and constant revision of some 40 pages of the club's manual, *Normal Operating Procedures and Emergency Action Plan* and the assembly of a Roles and Responsibility document. The committee has to keep abreast of current Health and Safety legislation and conduct regular risk assessment exercises. Some committee members and also some superintendents have attended risk assessment courses for this reason. An asbestos register is now mandatory. Fire extinguishers and smoke detectors have to be kept in top condition and electrical certification has to be obtained for electrical wiring and all appliances that employees use. In recent years the law on child protection has called for a new tier of bureaucracy and the club is obliged to vet its employees for suitability for contact with children. The importance of child protection can be judged by the 38-page document on child protection that was issued in 2003 by the NSPCC (National Society for the Prevention of Cruelty to Children) and the existence of the *Journal of Sexual Aggression* which publishes research into the sexual harassment and abuse of children.

The committee members and the superintendents need protecting too; con-frontations can occur at the gate with would-be gate crashers and verbal abuse with high attendant excitement is not unknown. Then there is the mother who rings the superintendents requesting that her son be sent home for his piano lesson and the following week the son requests permission to ring for his mother to come home to take him for his piano lesson. And one day a lady walked down the drive after seeing the banner over the entrance gate and asked one of the authors if there was a heated swimming pool . . .

Annual Reports and Financial Statements are created for the AGM (always poorly attended) and an occasional newsletter is produced, reviving thoughts of the 1930s club newsletter *The Tough Nut*. Featured amongst the items of business at the monthly meetings of the executive committee are the monthly account sheet and the allocation of money for both large (superintendents' remuneration) and small (tools and toasters) items. These meetings last for between two and three hours and are distinct from sub-committee meetings which plan and organise events or research and oversee specific projects. Dealing with membership renewals and applications is an annual exercise undertaken by a team of volunteers that is convened for the purpose. A computer was bought in 1998 to assist in the processing and keeping of records just 23 years after the then Hon. Treasurer bought his first hand-held calculator.

The maintenance of adequate insurance cover is another on-going necessity. The complexities of setting up satisfactory insurance cover for swimmers, anglers and the club's buildings has exercised committee members to an increasing extent year by year. Recently the authors were approached by an outfit called The Legal Advice Bureau which wished to know if 'you or any of your family have had an accident'. What is behind this hardly needs to be explained in these litigious times and it emphasises the importance of adequate liability cover plus ensuring that there is no possibility of negligence on the part of the club.

It is droll to recall that as late as the 1950s no one worried too much about the likelihood of having an accident, avoiding or preventing one; responsibility was on the individual. We have mentioned elsewhere the plethora of courses available to club committee members and employees and the fact that the club funds course attendances out of revenue. In 2000 the club commissioned a detailed report by RoSPA (Royal Society for the Prevention of Accidents) on its operation and activities. The results have been taken seriously and whenever or wherever a risk is identified action is taken and diligently recorded.

In 1991 the 10 metre diving platform was permanently closed in response to the FINA (Féderation International Natation) tables which list minimum recommended depths of water below diving towers and spring boards. For a 10 metre diving platform the FINA tables list 4.50 metres (14 ft 9 ins) as the minimum depth of water at plummet, and 5.00 metres (16 ft 5 ins) as the recommended depth. When the lake is full of water, i.e. up to edging flag stones, then the depth at plummet is 15 ft 9 ins but extended hot dry weather can actually reduce this to as little as 11 ft, even jeopardising the use of lower stages. The boards on the top stage and the steps leading up to it were therefore removed on recommendation of the trustees. The final blow of complete removal of the top structure has been resisted by die hards who cherish its decorative value and hope that one day it can be used again. While it was still in use deep dives occasionally touched a metre or so of sludge or slimy mud in the pit below the tower.

The closure was therefore forced upon us despite the fact that a 10 metre platform was in satisfactory use at Henleaze Lake for 70 years, where some of the finest high diving in the country has been seen (Fig. 4.11). The real rub came when RoSPA recommended that there should be no swimming at all in inland open waters. This resulted in the formation of the Rivers and Lakes Swimming Association, notably by Rob Fryer of the Farleigh and District Swimming Club and author of a directory of so-called wild swimming places. He is assisted, particularly on the legal side by Yacov Lev. The Association, of which Henleaze Swimming Club

Fig. 4.11 A swallow dive performed from the 10 metre high platform at Henleaze Lake by an unknown diver. Some of the finest high diving in the country has been seen at the lake during the 70 years that a 10 metre platform was in use and before Health and Safety considerations forced its closure. This photograph dates from the 1930s and was found by chance during a house clearance. Notice the lime kiln at the right behind the wooden diving tower. (photo unknown)

is a member, aims simply to preserve the joys of wild swimming and diving for this and future generations. The RLSA has a web site which can be accessed through a link on the Henleaze Swimming Club site (page 87).

The club property actually comprises of more land than water and the maintenance and improvement of the landed part has exercised successive generations of club officers. In 1938 Major Badock gave six weeping willow trees to the club and supervised their planting. All of these fine old trees still grace the club property in 2006 despite drought and surgery (Colour Fig. 4.15). After World War Two a number of ornamental trees and flowering shrubs were planted out – see Appendix 2. A 1946 shopping list with 36 items on it has survived in the archives. This exercise has been repeated down through the years, culminating in 2005 with the planting of many bulbs.

And So To The Future

Ultimate responsibility for the Henleaze Lake property and the club's future is legally vested in the trustees who are helped by the Executive Committee of which they are *ex officio* members. The trustees are a self perpetuating body of between two and four persons which was set up under the terms of the deed dated 12 May 1933 when the club purchased the 'Quarryland part of which is covered by water and used as a private bathing lake known as Henleaze Swimming Lake'. The Quarryland which was purchased is about 3.6 hectares (9.0 acres) in extent and the area covered by water is some 1.35 hectares (3.3 acres). The deed defines the trustees' powers and it is framed to ensure that the property shall be safe-guarded for the use and enjoyment of present and future generations of Henleaze Swimming Club members to whom the property belongs. Indeed, trustees have always been chosen for their love of the lake in its Arcadian setting and their determination to keep it as a pleasant, peaceful place only 5 km (3 miles) from the centre of Bristol.

A measure of the success achieved in preserving the club property intact and unchanged is given by the amazement and delight expressed by elderly one-time members who look in after decades of living elsewhere (cp Fig 4.12 on page 99). Success in preserving the property intact is also revealed by the variety of flowers, birds, trees and animal life to be found thriving there; the species observed since 2000 are listed in Appendix 2. Some of the birds are transient visitors, to be sure, but there is a rich resident population too.

The trustees, in particular, have also been instrumental in upholding the club's aims and charter. They have been able to act firmly to the benefit of the club in times of crisis. In 1958 the City Council's intention to fill in the northern half of the lake was averted and in 1960 the trustees managed to persuade the City Council to construct a massive steel fence around the northern end of the lake. More recently the trustees have been adamant that no non-swimming juniors, including babies should be allowed on to the club's premises (except for the purposes of taking the swimming test).

Since 2003 the trustees have also insisted on the principle that no club employee is permitted to serve on the Executive Committee. This ensures that committee members not only serve the club membership but are seen to be serving the club rather than seeking their own financial gain. The absence of vested interest in all committee members is important if the club membership at large is to have faith in, and respect for, the people who say what goes. When club management starts to pay itself, the club can become a commercial venture and the management committee is open to disinterest and, worse, corruption. The absence of paid employees on the committee also ensures that matters of employee pay and bonuses, and employee shortcomings can be discussed without inhibition. We may also note that there could be a hard-working honorary committee member who finds it invidious that one of his or her colleagues is being paid. The club's Rule 5 provides that the election of officers and the Executive Committee is subject to the approval of the trustees and indeed the trustees formally approve every new committee at its first meeting of the year in January.

We have touched on some of the things that fall short of the ideal, most of which have been unavoidable – the demise of water polo at the lake, the loss of club gala days, and the limitations imposed on high diving, especially by closure of the 10 metre high diving platform. Perhaps a future generation will see its way to excavating a deeper pit under the diving tower so that high diving can be seen at the lake again whatever the water level and whatever the FINA tables dictate.

We have also described how fishing at Henleaze Lake has grown since the swimming club's inception and there is no doubt that the lake has provided a well-used community facility in this respect. Fishing was also instrumental in stopping the practice of attempting to chlorinate the lake water, the presence of anglers day and night demonstrably arrested a serious intruder problem and fishing revenue has not been insignificant in helping to run and maintain the entire lake property.

Earlier we described how the club's championship events have increasingly been held away from the lake and how this culminated in the launch on 1 January 1993 of the separate club called Bristol Henleaze Swimming Club. Seven years later, the cups and trophies owned by Henleaze Swimming Club were awarded to champions for the last time. Colour Fig. 4.10 shows some of the members of the club's 2006 Executive Committee grouped around the club's cups (cp Colour Fig 1.4). These cups and trophies are now in storage and BHSC covers all competitive activities and training, awarding its own cups and trophies.

One of the club cups was taken out of storage in 2006 and applied to the competitive plunging competition that is held every year during the mid-summer party (Colour Fig. 4.13). A renaissance in open water competition swimming is actually occurring and Henleaze Swimming Club has not been slow to take part in it. Thus we have mentioned the introduction of the Gloucester County ASA Open Water Swimming Championship events that have been held at the lake annually since 1999 and the use of the lake by BHSC and BadTri for training purposes. One hopes that the future will bring more open water competitive swimming to Henleaze, perhaps even at Western Counties and National level once again.

The theme of this book has been never to lose sight of the past in the present. In this way the unchanging nature and spirit of the club and its property is retained as far as is possible against the formidable pressures of the times. Occasionally pre-war

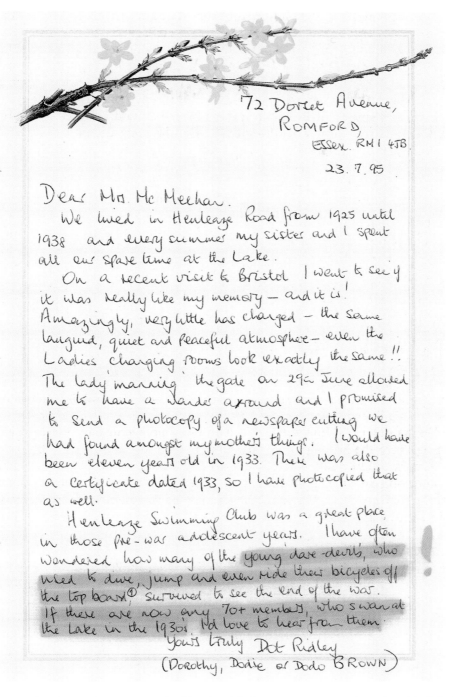

72 Dorset Avenue,
ROMFORD,
Essex. RM1 4JB.

23. 7. 95.

Dear Mrs. Mc Meehan.

We lived in Henleaze Road from 1925 until 1938 and every summer my sister and I spent all our spare time at the Lake.

On a recent visit to Bristol I went to see if it was really like my memory — and it is! Amazingly, very little has changed — the same languid, quiet and peaceful atmosphere — even the Ladies changing rooms look exactly the same!! The lady 'manning' the gate on 29th June allowed me to have a wander around and I promised to send a photocopy of a newspaper cutting we had found amongst my mother's things. I would have been eleven years old in 1933. There was also a certificate dated 1933, so I have photocopied that as well.

Henleaze Swimming Club was a great place in those pre-war adolescent years. I have often wondered how many of the young dare-devils, who used to dive, jump and even ride their bicycles off the top board, survived to see the end of the war. If there are now any 70+ members, who swam at the Lake in the 1930s, I'd love to hear from them.

Yours truly Dot Ridley
(Dorothy, Dodie or Dodo BROWN)

Fig. 4.12 This poignant letter was received by the club from a pre-war member who visited the lake after an absence of 57 years. It expresses nostalgic sentiments that the authors have heard from a remarkable number of pre-war members who are still around. At least two of them have reached 100 years of age. Swimming is evidently good for longevity as is having a good time at the lake.

Fig. 4.13 This certificate was issued in 1933 to Dorothy Brown, the writer of the letter in Fig. 4.12. Facsimile reproductions of this certificate have been offered to all swimmers who accomplish the so-called 'long swim' of at least 220 metres at the lake. The 'long swim' is a fun swim held twice a year.

Fig. 4.14 Ruth Moreton née Gardiner, a pre-war swimming member and one time Hon. Assistant Treasurer is still a regular member (the oldest?) at the time of writing. Here she examines archival photographs in the club house in 1999 during the club's 80th Birthday Celebrations. She was present at the club gala in 1935 when Pete Desjardins performed specimen dives. A permanent exhibition of old and contemporary photographs is maintained in the club house. (photo Derek Klemperer)

members visit the lake from afar and they are amazed to find that the place where they had the time of their lives is still essentially just as it was. The letter from one old timer expressing these sentiments is shown in Fig. 4.12 and her 1933 certificate of achievement is reproduced as Fig. 4.13. It is planned to continue running the lake in the same way as of old and to keep its time capsule appeal.

Shooting of the film *Nectar* at the lake in 2005 with a complete make-believe 1931 setting panders to this nostalgia, as does the occasional screening of the film that was made in 1935 when the Olympic gold medalist Pete Desjardins performed exhibition dives at the lake. A permanent exhibition of past and present photographs in the club room also helps to keep this theme on track (Fig. 4.14); it intrigues old and young members alike. How long we shall continue to post the water temperature every day in degrees Fahrenheit (as well as Celsius) and still exact the mandatory swimming test for membership of swimming a distance of 50 yards (Club Rule 11) instead of metres remains to be seen.

It seems to be likely that in the future more of the workload in running the club will have to be paid for. New tasks are being required of the committee members, some of whom are already overstretched. The monthly committee meetings tend to take longer and longer, occasionally exceeding three hours to get through the business in hand. At a time when the voluntary labour is shrinking, new administrative work has to be taken on board to cope with government legislation on Health and Safety and Child Protection, on employees' tax and records, on avoiding identity fraud, on access for the disabled, and so on.

Until 1997 membership records were dealt with by one committee member. Membership numbers have now reached record levels and a team is convened to process renewals. In 2007 the club's Hon. Treasurer Ross Harley installed the credit card method of making payments.

There is also an increasing tendency for maintenance work and construction projects to be undertaken by outside contractors. A part-time groundsman was employed for the first time in 2005. Nevertheless Henleaze Swimming Club is still far from a commercial business. Its real content and strength is based on the input, actions, and involvement of many volunteers who either hold down work elsewhere or are retired.

One of the formidable pressures that the trustees and the committee members have increasingly to address concerns liability. This will surely lead to the club becoming a company limited by guarantee in due course. Becoming a company is a logical step towards the club becoming a registered charity with all the financial advantages that this will entail. The trustees and committee therefore keep a watching brief on changes to charitable status law and any changes that come before parliament. Whether or not Henleaze Swimming Club will apply to the charity commissioners to become a charity in the fullness of time remains to be seen.

APPENDIX 1
PRESIDENTS OF
HENLEAZE SWIMMING CLUB

1919–1920	Col. George A. Gibbs, M.P.
1921	Maj. Stanley H. Badock, J.P.
1922	Albert G. Wain
1923	Arthur P. Furze
1924	William Scantlebury
1925	R.D. Kidd
1926	Horace Walker, D.L., J.P.
1927	George H. Chivers
1928	George Edwards
1929	Lt. Col. H.T. Curley, D.L.
1930	F.E. Metcalfe
1931	W.M. Good
1932	W.H. Parr
1933	Prof. John F. Dobson, M.A.
1934	Cecil F. Clark
1935	C. Sefton Cross
1936	Dr. C.J. Campbell Faill
1937	G.S. Reid
1938	John A. Bobbett
1939	L.W.W. Davis
1940–1945	The War Years
1946–1947	Reginald A. Macfarlane
1948	Vic H. Rands
1949	J. McCulloch
1950	S.W. Robinson
1951	Frederick W. Allard
1952	Eric S. Holdsworth
1953–1954	H.B. Smith
1955	E.A. Jennings
1956	F.C. Woolls
1957	Miss M.E. Cartridge
1958	Archie A. Macfarlane
1959	Wing Comm. R.A. Belcher
1960	Arthur T. Elliott
1961	W.J. Gordon
1962	A.G. Sergent
1963	Dr. F. Morgan
1964	F.J. Barron

1965	W. O. Vokins
1966–1967	Mrs Gwen Stephens
1968	Robert W. Steel
1969	Ernest A. Iles
1970–1971	Mrs Maisie B. Iles
1972	Frederick W. Allard
1973–1974	Dr. C. W. Mahood
1975–1977	John H. White
1978–1979	Mrs A. T. Elliott
1980–1981	Robert J. Teesdale
1982–1983	Dr. Derek F. Klemperer
1984–1985	Mrs Carol A. Holloway
1986–1987	Mrs Margaret M. Phillips
1988–1989	Jock Hutchings
1990–1991	Kenneth Mitchell
1992–1994	Mrs Joyce F. Klemperer
1995–1997	Grahame Moss
1998–2000	Mervyn Rowles
2001–2003	Mrs Margaret Golightly
2004–2007	Dr. Richard W. Spence

APPENDIX 2
FLORA AND FAUNA AT
HENLEAZE LAKE

Land Flora
(Bob Teesdale)

Bluebell
Bristol Flower
Buttercup
Columbine
Common Violet
Cotoneaster
Cow Parsley
Cowslip
Cranesbill
Crocus
Cuckoo Spit
Daffodil
Daisy
Dandelion
Deadly Nightshade
Forget-me-not
Foxglove
Hawkweed
Herb Robert
Hogweed
Honesty
Honeysuckle
Isis
Ivy
Knapweed
Ladies Smock
Lesser Celendine
Old Man's Beard
Ox-eye Daisy
Primrose
Ragwort
Red Campion
Red Clover
Red Valerian

Land Flora
(continued)

Rose, Dog
Rose, Guelder
Silver Weed
Snakes Head
Snowdrop
Toadflax
Tufted Vetch
Violet
White Deadnettle
Wood Avens

Water Flora
(Environment Agency)

Canary Grass
Fringed Lily
Greater Reedmace
Hornwort
Juncus Rushes
Lesser Reedmace
Phragmites
Purple Loosestrife
Sedge
Sweet Flag
Water Mint
Water Starwort
Waterlily, White
Waterlily, Yellow
Yellow Flag Iris

Trees
(Tony Titchen)

Apple
Ash
Birch, Silver
Birch, Silver (weeping crown)
Cherry, Bird
Cherry, Common
Elderberry
Elm, English
Elm, Wych
Field Maple
Hawthorn, Common
Hawthorn, Midland
Hazel
Horse Chestnut
Indian Bean Tree or Catalpa
Laburnum
Oak, English
Oak, Holm
Oak, Lucomb (hybrid)
Pear
Plum, Myrobalan
Plum, Yoshino Cherry (purple)
Privet
Rowan or Mountain Ash
Spindle
Sycamore
Wayfarer Tree
Whitebeam, Bristol
Whitebeam, Swedish
Willow, Golden Weeping
(hybrid)
Willow, White
Yew

Animals	Birds
	Birds
Badger	Barn Owl
Cat	Blackbird
Field Mouse	Bullfinch
Fox	Chaffinch
Frog	Common Bat
Grass Snake	Common Buzzard
Grey Squirrel	Coot
Hedgehog	Cormorant
Newt	Crow
Rat	Dove
Slow Worm	Duck
Toad	Dunnock
	Falcon
	Goose, Canadian
Fish	Goose, Chinese
(Colin Hannan)	Heron
	Jackdaw
Bream	Jay
Carp, Common	Kestrel
Carp, Crucian	Kingfisher
Carp, Khoi or Ghost	Little Glebe
Carp, Leather	Magpie
Carp, Linear	Mallard
Carp, Mirror	Mandarin Duck
Chubb	Moorhen
Eel	Pheasant
Perch	Pigeon, Feral
Pike	Pigeon, Ringed
Roach	Robin
Rudd	Sea Gull
Tench	Sparrow Hawk
	Swan
	Tawny Owl
	Thrush
	Tit, Blue
	Tit, Long Tailed
	Woodpecker, Green
	Woodpecker, Lesser Spotted
	Wren

NAME INDEX

SUBJECT INDEX

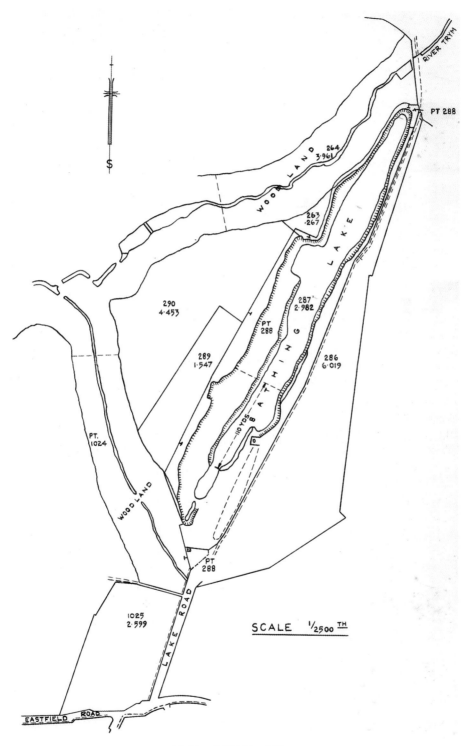

12 May 1933 Deed Plan

113

Friday Early Morning Swim

Starts Friday 1st June

Lake open from 7.15 am Fridays in June, July and August

 # Triathlon Training Session

Starts Sunday 13th May

10am - 11am Sundays in May, June, July and August

 # Mid Summer Tea Party

Choir

Saturday 23rd June 2.30pm to 9pm

The Henleaze Lake Story book launch , The Gasworks Singers, plunge competition, tea and cakes, late opening.

Gloucester County ASA 2007 Open Water Championship

Sunday 15th July 11.00am to 3pm

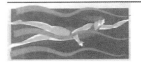 # Long Swim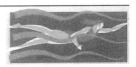

Sunday 8th July 3pm to 5pm
Diving stages will be closed during long swim